The Sin Blue Line

How God delivered me from the LAPD
And other miracles

Barry Q. Brooks J.D.

ISBN 978-1-63575-672-2 (Paperback)
ISBN 978-1-63575-673-9 (Digital)
ISBN 978-1-63575-674-6 (Hard Cover)

Christian Faith Publishing, Inc.
296 Chestnut Street
Meadville, PA 16335
www.christianfaithpublishing.com

Printed in the United States of America

Contents

Foreword 5

Background...9

God's Calling 15

The First Miracle..19

The Streets of LA 24

Another Miracle..28

A Christian Terrorist? 36

Career Taking Off 41

The Boards..52

The Noose Tightens 57

How Much Longer, Lord? 62

Two Miracles..66

The Lord Finally Speaks.......................................74

The First Prophet 82

The False Prophet...85

The Class Action 92

The Attack on My Family 106

The Prelude..113

Two Weddings and a Funeral 123

A Future Promise from God..138

Saved from Afghanistan..149

The "Dorner" Effect...172

Getting Out of God's Way 175

Am I Going to Die?..188

The Future 197

About the Author 200

Foreword: Why Write This Book?

◆ ◆ ◆ ◆ ◆

The Lord commissioned me to write this book and put it on my heart. He put a spiritual burden on me to get it completed and done for one purpose which I will explain in a moment. The idea of this book first came to me when I was in prayer and meditation in the Word about three o'clock in the morning. Although I had been in academia for sixteen years at the time and had contracted to write many different college level courses and curriculum, I had never really wanted to write a book—especially in the subject of soteriology. Personally, there are just way too many books written by pastors and other "experts" that are way off doctrine-wise and just lead people down the wrong path. *Just give me the Bible* was my mantra.

The Lord has always shown me extra kindness in giving me direction for things He wants me to accomplish. So when He told me it was His will for me to write this book, He was also gracious enough to give me confirmation. After putting it on my heart to write this book, I knew this would be a long and difficult task, full of emotion as well as time-consuming. I asked the Lord, *Lord, if you really want me to write this book, please give me absolute confirmation by the end of the week.* By the end of the week, I had four different confirmations from four different people. They were all unsolicited. I was at Church talking to a pastor about some of the things God was doing in my life and he said spontaneously, "You should write a book about your life." The next day, I was talking with my neighbor who is not a Christian and who usually avoids me and I was telling him about some of the things I had gone through with LAPD and he looked right at me and said, "You should write a book about your life." This happened two other times by the end of the week, giving me four words of confirmation from four different people—two Christians, two non-Christians.

After toiling for a year and only getting fifteen pages completed, I felt a tremendous burden to get it done. I told the Lord that I needed about $20,000 to pay for the work I would have to put aside in order to complete the book and also complete some well-needed repairs to my home that needed to be completed in order to dedicate time strictly to writing this book. I also knew it would be difficult as it was summer and all four of my young children would be playing loudly around my home office. The Lord arranged it so that I came into some unexpected money. In fact, after praying for $20,000, less than a week earlier, I received an anonymous check in the mail for $20,923.00. At the same time, my wife suddenly decided to take all four of my kids to the East Coast to visit a bunch of my relatives, many whom my kids had never met. This gave me three weeks of solitude in my home and my office in my house which is what I needed to get some work done. I was able to crank out fifty pages as inspired by the Holy Spirit and get the majority of the book completed. Then, after writing about seventy pages, a few months went by and it was now October and I had been thinking about the whole process. I had spent the last few weeks asking the Lord the same thing, *Why did you bring me three thousand miles from home (Massachusetts) to a place (Los Angeles) where I knew no one and give me a career only to take it away and give me twenty-five years of both extreme hardship but also some incredible spiritual revelations along the way and then write a book about all of it?* A few days later, I was filling up my car with gas getting ready to drive to work to give a lecture at the university and that exact thought went through my mind. I heard God say to me loudly, not vocally, but very clear and concise and unmistakably—"*For My glory*" he said. I thought, *For His glory?* I was contemplating that revelation while getting back in my car after finishing pumping the gas. As soon as I sat in my car and turned it on, the radio came on which was tuned to a local Christian radio station called KWAVE. There was a program in progress and the pastor, whose name I forget, was in the middle of a sermon and these are the first words I heard when the radio came on: "And we do these things for His glory." I knew I had my confirmation. Once again, God had proven himself faithful in giving me confirmation in what He knew would be a long and emotional journey of recounting more than twenty-five years of hardship, but more so, God's miracles and interventions in my life to serve as an inspiration of God's faithfulness to those that cry out "Abba Father." The result is the book you are now holding.

Background

I remember when God first called me into police work. Now I wasn't saved until I was twenty-three years old when I gave my life to Christ, but I always knew from early childhood that God had predestined me to serve Him (Romans 13). I was nine years old when my paternal grandfather passed away. I didn't know too much about him except to say that his first wife had died at a very young age and he had remarried to my step-grandmother Chloe. I was asked by my parents if I wanted to go to the funeral but I declined. I was nine and didn't have a concept of death but a funeral sounded boring.

It was a few years later when I was visiting my step-grandmother, now widowed, that I saw a picture of my grandfather up on a shelf in the living room dressed as a police officer. I must have been thirteen or fourteen years old. Many young boys growing up often talk about growing up to be police officers, firefighters, doctors, etc. However, that picture of my grandfather in uniform stuck with me and as I went into high school and started to prepare for college and a career. It was cemented in my spirit that I would become a police officer and serve God and people in this way. Little did I know that my career would eventually take me three thousand miles away.

I have to be honest and say that I wasn't a very good student in high school. I was lucky enough to play football for North Reading High School. They never won a championship until my first year in high school when I was on Junior Varsity. High school back then was only three years—sophomore, junior, and senior years only. Freshmen was still a part of junior high school or, as they say on the West coast, middle school. All three years that I played football, we won the league championship and even went to the division three super bowl my junior year. Being from a very small and traditional town in the suburbs of Massachusetts, everyone was out rooting for us. Parents let their daughters stay out later if she was with a football player; boys who were not on the team envied us. Every Friday night after the film session, we would walk out of the high school gymnasium around nine in the evening and about two dozen parents would be waiting for us with donuts and hot chocolate (This was New England in the Fall/Winter). So during my three years in high school, those of us that played football had social status and recognition. None of my brothers played any organized sports in high school so when I played football, my dad became excited about watching one of his sons play sports. He was always at my games come rain or snow. I wish I played more. I was a pretty good tight end/receiver with good hands and decent speed (I ran track). However, my junior year, I was converted to a down lineman. A position in which I was about forty pounds too small for. However, I was just happy to contribute and be on a team that went 26-1-1 in my three years there.

The importance of academia was not really pushed upon me and my two brothers and two sisters. My mom and dad had no education beyond high school and didn't have a lot of money. I barely saw my father growing up because he worked two jobs back to back. He went to work at 6 a.m. and worked for the Town of North Reading Water Department. He would finish at 3:30 p.m. and come home for dinner and a quick one-hour nap. He would then go back to work from 6 p.m. until midnight mopping floors and picking up trash as a janitor. He would come home at midnight and get back up at 5:30 am to do it all over again the next day. One thing that I inherited from my father was his work ethic.

We didn't go to church growing up as a family. I would describe my parents as Universalists. They believed that when you died, if the good outweighed the bad, you would make it to heaven. David, my best friend growing up since the age of four, took me with his parents to a local church, the First Baptist Church of North Reading. I looked forward to vacation bible school each summer there.

However, it wasn't until I was twenty-three years old that I gave my life to Christ. I was actually driven to do this because I was distraught over my girlfriend at the time, who I wanted to marry but broke up with me. I was so upset that I drove to the First Baptist Church and found Pastor Terry and an Elder, Don Bell, who prayed with me in the pastor's office to receive Christ. Something happened to me at that moment. It wasn't a Damascus Road experience like the Apostle Paul had but all of a sudden my "eyes" were opened. All the partying, sex, alcohol that I had been doing which never bothered me a bit, now pricked my conscience. I was now astutely aware that when I continued doing these things that I was sinning against God. Maybe this is what happened when Adam and Eve first bit into the apple and their eyes were opened and they suddenly became aware of their nakedness for the first time.

I already felt God calling on me to go into law enforcement even before I was saved. I had strategically set a path for a successful career in law enforcement since the age of eighteen. When I was eighteen, there were two things I knew about my future: I needed a college education and I needed to get law enforcement experience. My parents didn't have the money to pay for college and my grades were not good enough for a scholarship. Also, you could not, by law, be a police officer until you were twenty-one years of age. However, there was one exception—the military. So I had to figure out how to go into the military and serve as a police officer while at the same time going to college. I looked around at different branches of the armed forces and decided that I didn't want to go active military and be in some foreign country or even a war for the next three years. So I started looking at reserves. I looked at the army, navy, air force, marines and even the coast guard. Then I discovered the Army National Guard. The Army National Guard was different from the Army Reserves in that you worked primarily for the governor of your state and not the president of the United States. They also had better college tuition programs and guaranteed my Military Occupation Specialty (MOS) as 95 Bravo military police.

Consequently, in August of 1981, two months after graduating high school, I left for basic training followed by military police academy in Fort McClellan, Alabama. After completing basic training and the military police academy, I was assigned to a military police company near my residence which was located in an armory inside Boston University. As an aside, I worked a security detail every year as a military police officer for the Boston Marathon and was stationed close to where the Tsarnaev Brothers would eventual set off their pressure cooker bombs causing mass casualties in 2013. I spent the next six years of my life in the military police. I patrolled military bases and federal compounds. I made arrests and investigated crimes. I got to work with Army Criminal Investigation Division (CID). Now CID was much like the television show that has been popular for the last decade or so called NCIS. I also was recruited to the SRT. The SRT or Special Reaction Team was the National Guard's version of a SWAT team.

Concurrently with serving in the military, I attended college. I started off with the local community college, Northern Essex Community College because quite honestly I did not have the grades to go directly to a four-year university. After a couple of years of majoring in criminal justice in community college, I transferred to Salem State College (Now Salem State University). During my two years at Northern Essex Community College, I got an internship with the Essex County Sheriff's Department. After the internship, they hired me to work as a corrections officer in a local county jail. In my last year at Salem State College, I became the first intern to be allowed inside the United States Marshals Service. As explained to me, it wasn't worth the time and effort to conduct a federal criminal background check on an intern who would be gone after one semester. This is why they didn't allow interns into sworn law enforcement positions. I would like to think that God had a hand in me being accepted to the US Marshals internship and He might have but I was just a baby Christian at the time and He hadn't revealed His purpose and plan for me yet (Jeremiah 29:11). The marshals experience was incredible. Most of the Deputy US Marshals were Vietnam veterans and did things the old fashion way. Because of my background in the Military Police and Sheriff's Department, they sponsored a carry conceal weapons permit (CCW) from the state of

Massachusetts. So I got to carry a handgun. In addition to signing warrants for asset and forfeiture seizure, I was sometimes allowed to go out on missions with some of the deputy marshals. In fact, we drove around in a BMW (if I recall correctly) that was confiscated from drug dealers in an asset and forfeiture deal involving a Jamaican Posey. So there I was, driving around Boston, armed with a Smith and Wesson 45 pistol, with two really cool but crazy veteran Deputy United States Marshals.

God's Calling

By the spring of 1988, everything in my plan for a successful law enforcement career was taking shape. I had earned two undergraduate degrees including having just graduated with my bachelor's degree in criminal justice from a very respectable college. I had completed my six-year obligation in the Army National Guard Military Police and had been given an honorable discharge. I had law enforcement employment experience with both the Essex County Sheriff's Department and the United States Marshals Service. My future looked very bright. The marshals wanted to hire me and sent me to FLETC (Federal Law Enforcement Training Center) to be trained and hired as a full-time Deputy U. Marshal. I had also just received a very high score on the Massachusetts State Police exam and was about to start that process. If you have ever seen the movie *The Departed* then you will understand how well respected the Massachusetts State Police are among law enforcement organizations. I had now been a Christian for two years and was struggling to figure out what that meant and learning how to live the Christian life. No one in my family was a Christian—not yet. So I had no real fellowship or mentorship and didn't know that I was supposed to start cultivating a relationship with my heavenly father. However, my career was about to take off. Then came the phone call.

Judy had been a friend of mine through junior high school and high school. She dated a friend of mine I had hung out with and played football with during those years. I had lost track of her after high school as I went into the military and to local college. In May of 1988, she called me out of the blue and asked me if I wanted to come visit her out in San Diego. She was attending The University of California at San Diego to become a chiropractor. I had never been to California before and actually had never been west of the Mississippi River. I imagined California was flat and hot much like my experiences living in Florida for three months during the summer of '85. I thought, "Why not?" I could check out San Diego and California and then come back and kick off my law enforcement career in Massachusetts with the State Police or with the United States Marshals Service. Surely this was God's plan for me. However, as it turns out, it was just mine.

I flew out to San Diego for a week to visit Judy. It was my second day there when Judy told me that she had to go to work the next day and would be gone the entire day. It was then that the Holy Spirit spoke to me. I had never directly heard from the Lord before— at least not that I was aware of. I had been a Christian for about two years but as I said before, I wasn't discipled or had been disciplined in establishing a relationship with the Lord or made too much of an effort of consistently getting into the Word and reading my Bible. I think one of the biggest mistakes postmodern Christians make is that they are not taught to develop a relationship with the Lord and be able to recognize His voice when He speaks to us. This seems to be an anathema for Roman Catholics and orthodox Christians. I think God is constantly speaking to us but in many cases we haven't developed the patients and discipline as well as discernment to listen to Him. How many of our prayers consist of us kneeling down before bed time and rattling off a list of wants and needs to the Lord and then say "amen" and go to bed or back to watching television? Prayer becomes a monologue instead of a dialogue.

I can't say that I heard an actual voice from the Lord on my second day in San Diego, but suddenly I felt led by the Holy Spirit to rent a car the next day and drive up to Los Angeles which is about one hundred miles north of San Diego. What happens when you become "born again" as Jesus explains in Gospel of John 3:3, is that God sends the Holy Spirit to come live inside of you whose primary purpose is to conform you to be like Jesus. God is spirit and the born again believer has the spirit living inside him. Although we know that God does speak audibly as seen throughout the Old Testament as well as the New Testament as seen in Jesus' baptism and the transfiguration, God's spirit speaks to the spirit within us and from my experience it is just as clear and cogent as if it was audible—maybe more so. So I was told by the Lord to go to Los Angeles. This, of course, was in the days before cell phones, internet, Google maps, GPS or MapQuest. There were no digital navigational systems available. Just maps and Thomas Guides. Keep in mind that I had never been to California before and really had no idea where I was going. So the next day I rented a car and started toward Los Angeles around noon time. The only place I ever really heard of in the greater Los Angeles area was Hollywood. As I said, this was well before GPS and cell phones and Tom Toms, so I got the old Thomas Guide out and started planning a route. However, the Lord had not given me a specific destination in Los Angeles. He just told me to drive to Los Angeles and trust Him. I had no real plan to see any tourist sites or go to any particular attraction but I just felt drawn by God to come to Los Angeles. During the course of the drive, I was having a conversation with God as I drove down the freeway. I was talking to the Lord about what His plan and purpose was for me (Jeremiah 29:11). I knew that I would have a choice of a couple of law enforcement opportunities when I got back home to North Reading, MA. I arrived somewhere in the Los Angeles vicinity around two or three in the afternoon. Around five I started driving down Venice Boulevard not really knowing where I was going. After getting lost for a while and then getting back on to Venice Boulevard I came to a stop sign at the intersection of Venice Boulevard and Longwood Avenue. All of a sudden I heard the Lord tell me to stop. Then another command to look up. I immediately looked up and saw that I was in front of the Los Angeles Police Department's Wilshire Division. There was a big yellow banner hanging across the building that said, "LAPD now hiring. Written exam given every Tuesday at 7 p.m." It was already Tuesday at 6:45 pm. I pulled over and began to mull this over. Was this God directing me? I had no plans to leave Massachusetts and certainly none that included coming to California in which I knew only one person in the entire state who lived a hundred miles away. I just felt convicted to follow through with what was in front of me. I walked inside and presented my driver's license. After a brief introduction by an officer, I was given the written test which lasted an hour. I passed the test with flying colors, but now what? I was only in town for five more days before flying back home. Just then I was approached by an LAPD recruiter who asked me where I was from. I told him Massachusetts. After telling him a little bit about my background, he opined that I would make a good cop and that it just so happens that they (LAPD) started a new pilot program for those recruits who were from out of state. This new program allowed those from outside California to complete all seven steps of the hiring process in four days. The written test, oral interview, physical fitness test, written psychological, oral psychological, initial background check, etc. Sensing God at work here, I went ahead and scheduled my oral interview for the next day. As explained to me, if I didn't pass the oral interview, I wouldn't be allowed to continue on with the rest of the hiring process. It was further told to me by the recruiter that because I was white (Caucasian), I would need to get a score of at least 95/100 on the interview. It was explained to me that LAPD was under a federal consent decree to prioritize the hiring of minorities and females. So females needed a score of 75/100 to pass the oral interview and male blacks or Hispanics needed and 85/100. However, male whites needed above ninety-five to be considered for further processing. This was my first encounter with affirmative action. I ended up scoring high enough to process further and passed every subsequent test they threw at me.

Needless to say, I left California five days later with a conditional job offer contingent upon my completed background history being done. By July of 1988, I had been confirmed for an LAPD academy date of September 12, 1988. However, I was told that this date was not static and I wouldn't really know for sure until about two weeks before the academy class started.

The First Miracle

✦ ✦ ✦ ✦ ✦

I flew back to my home town in North Reading still buzzing about what had just taken place. Los Angeles? Could this really be God's will for my life? I started doing some research on the Los Angeles Police Department and came away impressed. They were widely considered the best municipal law enforcement agency in the country (at least before Rodney King). They had practically invented SWAT and the DARE (Drugs Awareness Resistance Education) and were highly disciplined. Very paramilitary. I was told that they only accept one out of every fifteen hundred applicants. The streets of Los Angeles were another matter. The introduction of crack cocaine into America's urban centers along with an explosion of juvenile population and youth gang activity proved to be a volatile mix. Los Angeles was leading the country in drive by shootings, gang related homicides, and juvenile homicides.

My parents inherited a cottage up in Pugwash, Nova Scotia from my maternal grandparents. It was located in a small fishing village on the edge of the Atlantic Ocean in the Canadian Maritime Providences. The cottage was ninety miles from the nearest major town and airport and the last part of the journey is small winding roads with no shoulders and no street lights. They don't even plow the roads in the winter. It gets so cold that the ocean located just thirty feet from the front door of the cottage would freeze solid by January. Instead of shoulders on the edges of the roads, many of the roads just dropped off into eight to ten foot gullies. The distance from my house in North Reading, Massachusetts to our cottage in Nova

Scotia is roughly about seven hundred miles. It is a very long drive (about fourteen hours) through Massachusetts, New Hampshire, Maine, New Brunswick and Nova Scotia. A very rural area. I had recently purchased a motorcycle from a neighbor for the first time in my life. I had been riding a short time when I decided to visit my parents at the cottage in Nova Scotia in July of 1988—eight weeks prior to my LAPD Academy start date. I drove my motorcycle pretty much fourteen hours straight through, stopping a couple times for gas and food. I hit a couple of rainstorms on the way and got pretty soaked. I got there after night fall and the temperature had dropped significantly. Between the cold and being a human sponge, I started to become hypothermic. My parents wrapped me in blankets and put a heating pad on me. During the evening, I was able to shake off the shivers and by morning I was feeling better. Little did I know that the Lord was about to do a miracle in my life.

That afternoon I decided to take my motorcycle for a drive. I was coming back from town in a patch of road that had deep trenches on both sides and was heavily wooded. I was going about 50 mph when I came to a sudden extreme bend in the road. I could not manipulate the turn and went off the road and into the deep gully that runs parallel to the road. Suddenly I was running head long into a brick wall that was part of a driveway that acted as a solid bridge across the gully for the driveway but a six-foot-deep solid wall for me. I hit the brick wall at about 40 mph and the force of the impact threw me off the motorcycle. I was launched airborne and actually hurdled the entire width of the driveway just missing splattering my head on a telephone phone. I landed after what seemed like an eternity in the gully on the other side of the driveway. When I hit the ground, the impact knocked all of the wind out of me and I gave out a huge *oooof!* For a split second, I started to think I had just survived something that should have killed me, and then I saw it. Out of my peripheral vision I saw a glimpse of the motorcycle as it was about to land on me. Apparently, it liked to fly as well and had leaped that walled partition of a driveway and cleared the driveway. I don't really remember the impact, just bracing for the imminent thud. When I woke up, the first thing I remember was that my back felt numb. I looked up and could see the top of the gully and the clouds overhead. *No one would ever find me down here*, I thought. I am not visible from the road and there was very little traffic on this road. The first thought that came to me was that they won't find me until the spring thaw. Then I tried to get up but I couldn't. I looked at my legs as if to say to them apparently you didn't get the order. I tried several times to stand up until I realized I was paralyzed from the waist down. So now I faced the challenge of getting out of an eight to ten-foot ditch that was muddy and unstable with just upper body strength. I clawed at the side of the ditch and tried to pull myself up which proved difficult because the soil was wet and unstable. Whenever I dug my hands into the side of the wall, the dirt would give way and crumble. Eventually, after what seemed like forever, I was able to crawl and wiggle my upper body all the way to the top of the gully and on to the edge surface of the road. I still had a couple of problems. First, this was a lone country road very little travelled so the chances of someone coming along and helping soon were slim. Second, this was back in the days before cell phones so I couldn't call 911 or Canada's equivalent of it.

So here I was laying on the side of the road, somewhere in the Maritime providences, paralyzed from the waist down, about two months before I was supposed to start my career with the Los Angeles Police Department. I started talking to the Lord about His newly revealed plans for my life three thousand miles from home and how being paralyzed would certainly put a damper in His plans before it started. I am of the belief that if God clearly speaks to His children and often gives us a promise through prophecy or word of knowledge (which is how this book got written). God speaks to us sometimes directly, sometimes through another person, through circumstances in our lives and in many cases, through His Word. When He tells us what He wants us to do, especially if it is very difficult or seems unreasonable in the flesh, He is very willing to confirm it so you know it was from Him. I hadn't asked for confirmation on this new plan to join LAPD because I was still young and inexperienced in the faith and it seemed so obvious given the chain of events that it was from the Lord. My experience has also been that God sends trials into the lives of His saints in order to test them, strengthen them, and cause us to rely upon Him. Now I can look back over a twenty-five-year legacy of one miracle after another. However, this would prove to be my first real test in trusting God. Trusting Him in the present circumstances so that I would trust Him later to follow His plan to Los Angeles.

I laid along the roadside for a long time. Eventually, a pick-up truck came by and stopped when he saw the carnage. I don't remember too much about him. I told him I couldn't move my legs or get up and he picked me up and laid me in the back of the pick-up truck. As I lay there in the bed of the truck as it slowly twisted and winded its way through dirt roads and humid air, I started praying to God, *Lord, if your will is for me to go to Los Angeles and join the LAPD, then you need to heal me and do so quickly.* I can't say that I immediately felt warmth in my body or anything out of the ordinary. In fact, I really felt nothing. Trust. The Lord was telling me to trust Him and believe. This would be my first real test; one of many to come. I was still a baby Christian and even though I had been born again now for about two years, I really hadn't grown spiritually because I had no mentors or men in my life that were believers. I was very susceptible at this point to a lot of influence and I read a lot of books without wisdom or discernment which is dangerous. In fact, just two years prior to giving my life to Christ, out of my search for something meaningful, I dabbled with Scientology after reading the book *Dianetics*. Thank God He saved me from that cult. I should have just stuck with reading the Bible. I convinced my sister and brother-in-law who was staying at the cottage not to bring me to hospital (the nearest hospital being ninety minutes away). Instead they loaded me into their car to bring me back to my home in Massachusetts. By this time, I was as rigid as a board. My back had now completely seized up on me and they had to lay the front seat as far back as it would go so that it was almost parallel with the back seat. I had to lay across the seat that was set back at about 140-degree angle and endure a seven hundred mile ride back. Every single bump felt like a knife to the back.

The following day, I arrived home and my brother-in-law, Donnie, helped me to my bed. Everyone was still back in Pugwash at the cottage except my sister Julie who lived about twenty-five miles away with her husband Donnie and my brother Bobby who worked in Boston so wasn't around that much. It gave me a lot of quiet time to think and pray about the situation. Even though I couldn't walk, I felt hope. According to my LAPD background investigator, I would probably be slotted for a September academy class. Gradually, over the next few weeks, my back began to heal as I prayed and meditated on the word of God. By the time I received my notice in the middle of August that I was accepted into the LAPD Academy class of September 12, 1988, my back was almost completely healed. An x-ray taken a few years later would reveal a healed fractured spine. This is how I know the Lord did heal me. I did have one nagging residual effect from the motorcycle accident which was a broken foot. From day one in the police academy, we ran. We ran everywhere. We ran to our lockers, ran to class, often would do five mile runs during PT, ran anywhere and anytime we were on the LAPD Academy grounds. That was the rule. Every night I would go home and have to ice my fractured foot because it would swell up. However, there was no way I was going to be recycled. I saw them all the time, the recycles. A recruit who had been injured in the academy and couldn't keep up with his or her class and so had to be "recycled" in another class when healed. Often times, they bounce around performing administrative tasks in their recruit uniforms. Many of them eventually quit. No way was that happening to me. I bought a size 13 left running shoe (my injured foot) and a size 12 right shoe and sneaker so that I could keep pushing it through the academy and the extra space that one extra size made allowed for the swelling and edema to occur during the day without me having to remove the shoe.

The Streets of LA

C oming from a small New England town, I was oblivious to cultural diversity. I grew up in a state that was about 95% Caucasian and in a town that to my memory had no African-Americans in it. I don't remember ever even seeing an African-American individual in person until I was in boot camp in the Army in Alabama at the age of eighteen. It was quite a shock being thrown into South Central Los Angeles back in 1989 right out of the police academy during the peak of the gang wars. Once crack cocaine had been introduced into the urban centers of America, it became the perfect vehicle for gangs to feed on. Before crack came along, powdered cocaine was considered a rich man's drug, costing about $100 for a gram. It was a party drug that I saw show up in many frat parties during my undergrad years in college in the early 1980s. What made crack such a perfect drug for the poor and the socioeconomic underclass was that it was cheap. A typical "rock" of cocaine was only $10 and provided a much more intense high and euphoria leading to a much greater level of addiction. Crack cocaine, although prevalent in minority neighborhoods, didn't discriminate. It wasn't that uncommon for me in the predominately African-American projects to pull over a white women driving a $60,000 Volvo with an infant and toddler in the back seat. In fact, there was no other reason for her to be in the projects other than to purchase rock cocaine. It was tough to arrest a mother of two, take her kids to social services, tow the car away and now she is a felon. A lot different than arresting your typical user who is usually good for a dozen burglaries and break-ins of numerous automobiles in order to support their habit. A middleclass mom could just take an advance on her credit cards or raid their kid's college funds to support her addiction.

As discussed, I grew up in a state that was 95% white, in a town that was 100% white. Thus, when I came to Los Angeles, I had no preconceived ideas about African-Americans. Some police officers found it easy to label African-Americans as gangsters or as one of my partners use to call them "jungle bunnies." Day after day we dealt with Black-on-Black crime, a negative attitude toward police, and what seemed like a self-perpetuated socioeconomic concept of victimization. We got shot at a lot. It wasn't unusual to see fourteen-year-old kids riding small bicycles around neighborhoods with sawed off shotguns across the handle bars. So it was understandable that after spending a little time working the streets of Seventy-Seventh Division or South East or South West Division in South Central Los Angeles that an officer's opinion of African-Americans could become negative and may encumber a sinister attitude toward these people. Understandable but not acceptable. I was appalled at how the LAPD interacted with African-American citizens in South Central Los Angeles. I can recall one particular incident which I believe will act as a microcosm of treatment of African-Americans by the LAPD. It is an example I frequently use when teaching classes on ethics and cultural diversity at the University. One day, my partner and I heard a request for a back-up come out on a stolen car (code-37). A unit had run the license plate of an old brown Cadillac and it came back as stolen. Cadillacs seemed to be the vehicle of choice in predominantly African-American neighborhoods back then. We ended up behind the primary unit who had ran the vehicle's license plate and determined it was stolen. After the police helicopter (air unit) arrived overhead, the primary unit decided to stop the vehicle. This is always a tense time. By this time, the bad guys in the stolen car pretty much know you are on to them and they are waiting for the police lights and siren to sound so they can make their escape or start shooting or both. Concurrently, the police officers know that as soon as the lights and siren go on, the chase will start, often times putting their lives at great risk. This is why we usually wait to get a police helicopter overhead and a backup unit before we attempt to stop the vehicle. More times than not, the bad guys driving the stolen car will attempt to evade us by fleeing away at dangerous speeds and eventually crash and either a shooting or a foot pursuit will occur or both.

As soon as the primary unit activated its lights and siren, the driver of the vehicle slowly pulled over on the street. Standard protocol directed the primary unit to initiate a felony stop. On the public address system, the lead officer ordered the driver of the stolen vehicle out of the car with his hand up. As the driver's door slowly opened, out came a very elderly African-American man of about eighty years of age (I would later learn that he was a pastor of a local church). He was very frail, shaking, and obviously scared, and of little danger to anyone. He was ordered out into the middle of the street, down to his knees and then face down on the pavement, hand and legs spread out, palms up. I found it a little difficult to swallow that we were following protocol for a possibly armed and dangerous criminal on this old man who walked with a limp. Next, the passenger was ordered to exit via the driver's side door. Out, very gingerly, came an elderly African-American woman who was confused, frightened, and could barely walk unassisted. By this time, there were about six police officers pointing handguns at these folks. She too, was placed face down on the ground next to her husband in the middle of the street. By this time of course, many curious individuals, neighbors, and curiosity-seekers had come out of their homes or out of their cars since all traffic was stopped both ways, to see the commotion. Once all suspects were out of the vehicle, it was now my job as the secondary unit to walk up to the vehicle and tactically clear the vehicle for other persons lying in wait. As I approached the vehicle and was checking the trunk to make sure there wasn't a lay off guy to ambush us, I heard the officer who had broadcasted the original stolen car information call out a Code-4. I heard, "Code-4, this is not a stolen vehicle. I ran the wrong license plate." I looked back at my partner and training officer a little quizzical. He started waiving his hands at me in a come-here motion very rapidly. His face was expressing concern and he was anxious. Since I was the rookie and he was my training officer, I just did what I was told and ran back to the patrol car. My partner said, "Get in." As we did a quick 180-degree turn with the screeching of tires, I saw the primary unit already ahead of us speeding away. I looked up and saw the police helicopter making a sharp turn to the west and heading away at 60 knots. Out of curiosity, I looked back over my left shoulder and out the rear window of the police car at the elderly couple to see what was going on with them. I thought a supervisor would be explaining to them why the stop occurred or perhaps apologizing to them. What I saw was shocking. There, still lying in the middle of the street, was the elderly couple now abandoned, alone with no police nearby. I watched as they became smaller and smaller in my glance through the rear window and the elderly African-American man struggled to his knees and fell back down again.

Two things crossed my mind right away. The first was, *Why in the world do these people put up with us?* and *How can we treat these people this way?* The answer, as I soon learned, was based in utilitarianism. The LAPD was simply the lesser of two evils and a necessary one at that. As bad as we treated the African-American community, we were necessary to combat the ever increasing gang presence and violence that had taken hold of South Central Angeles. It would only be a few years later after the Rodney King incident that the African-American population would show their frustration with the LAPD by setting the city ablaze and looting and rioting. It was interesting to think that God had brought me three thousand miles to what seemed like a foreign city and vastly diverse culture in order to help change my perspective on people. It helped give me perspective on God's love which is color blind and is not limited to race, gender, ethnicity, or anything else. It was during my first year with LAPD, while working in South Central Los Angeles, that God supernaturally protected me.

Another Miracle

❖ ✦✦✦✦✦ ❖

I was assigned to the Seventy-Seventh Division Gang Task Force in 1989 and part of 1990. I mainly worked the Crip gangs such as the Rolling 60s, 83 (eight trey) gangsters, 83 Hoovers, etc. My partner was named Sam. Sam, who was African-American, was raised in South Central Los Angeles and often knew the people in the neighborhoods in which we were arrested gang members in. One night we were working a Z-car which is a specialized unit assigned to handle special problems that were either out of the expertise of patrol or that they simply did not have time to adequately address the problem due to the needs of handling radio calls for service. We heard a unit request for assistance that was in pursuit of a stolen vehicle with four gang members inside possibly armed. Within about two minutes, we became the secondary unit behind the primary unit. Normally, besides a backup unit, you want to wait for an airship police helicopter to get overhead. Nothing beats having eyes in the sky especially if it turns into a foot pursuit which it almost always does. The police helicopters, or airships as we call them, also had the forward looking infrared scopes (F.L.I.R.) so at nighttime they can see bad guys hiding in the dark, under trees, bushes, cars, etc. This is how they found one of the Boston Marathon bombers who was hiding in a covered boat. The pursuit had reached 89th street and had turned South on Towne Avenue. As we turned the corner in our police car, we saw the primary unit in front of us and that the vehicle we were pursuing had just crashed into a tree. As we were pulling up behind the primary unit, suddenly, four young African-American teens got out of the car and started running. One of the rules of foot pursuits is that you never separate from your partner. You always should be in line of sight of him. If your partner is slow, you don't rush ahead of him. When these four gangsters started running, two went straight down 89th and two ran past me and my partner and then turn and ran into the back yard of the house at the corner of 89th and Towne. For whatever reason, the two officers in the primary unit split up. One ran straight down 89th by himself and one rand the other gangster chasing him behind the house. My partner Sam joined this officer and ran with him in pursuit of the two gangsters that had ran to the back of the house, leaving the one officer alone to chase the two other gang members. I had to break protocol and pair up with the lone officer who ran after the other gangsters. This break in protocol probably saved my life. As my partner got into the backyard, he saw that the first suspect had gone over a wooden fence that separated the yard from another property and the second suspect was straddling the fence about to leap off into the darkness and the other side. My partner gave the command to freeze but the second suspect kept going over the fence. My partner started to climb the fence and was almost to the top when a hail of bullets let loose. Normally, I would have been with my partner and that would have been me going over the fence or I would be right *behind* him. I heard several gunshots. Then I heard another. Bullets seem to be coming from both sides of the fence. One bullet struck my partner in the heel area and spun him partially around while he was on the fence. Another bullet quickly penetrated his neck and he fell from the fence. The scene was total chaos. We had both 77th Division and Southeast division police officers arriving at the scene at the same time. Each division works on a separate radio frequency. Cops in the front yard didn't know that there were cops in the backyard (separated by the fence) and ended up shooting at each other. As my partner lay there mortally wounded (or so I thought at the time), every single fiber in my being wanted to destroy whoever had shot my partner and who had put my life in danger. I pulled out my service weapon I had holstered in anticipation of climbing the fence and aimed it at the place where the bullets were coming through the fence. I was going to empty my gun into that fence when all of a sudden I heard a voice. Not an audible voice but a distinct voice in my head that said *Can you see what you are shooting at?* I instantly harkened back to my LAPD academy days where the four universal safety rules of handling a firearm were drilled into my head. *Never point your gun at something you are not willing to destroy.* Of course, I couldn't see what I was shooting at so I did not pull the trigger. As it turns out, it was the two officers that had chased the first two gangsters down 89th street had pursued them around to the house next to an adjacent to the house and backyard where my partner was at. These officers started shooting at the suspects and the bullets that missed the suspects continued down range, striking my partner and almost killing him. So as it turns out, if I had shot back as my survival instincts were telling me, chances are, I may have shot or killed another police officer. This would not be the first time that God supernaturally protected me as I have been shot at and ambushed on a number of occasions. In fact, it would be only a month until God saved my life again.

The following month, November of 1989, I was still working the gang unit and my former partner who had been shot was resting in a convalescent hospital trying to re-learn how to walk again after one of the bullets lodged in his spine. Rumors began to abound that some intelligence had been gained that one of the gang-banger's girlfriend worked for the Department of Motor Vehicles and was trying to gain access to data bases on police officers who worked the gang unit to find out where they lived. There were also rumors that they were going to ambush us or place a pipe bomb under one of our unit's black and whites (police vehicles). We were a small unit of handpicked hard chargers that liked going after the gangsters. To me I didn't care about the danger. Too often I was being summoned to a call to see a young boy whose body was riddled with bullets laying out in the street. By the time we rolled up, word had gotten back to the boy's mother. Every mother's instinct is to protect her child. I am standing there over her child with a crowd around, ambulance pulling away after they pronounced the kid dead, looking at the body for signs of gang tattoos. Here comes mom screaming, "Not my baby, not my baby." One of the hardest things in the world is trying to keep mama from every maternal instinct she has which is to grab her child and try to hold him and shake him awake like it was a dream. However, that body is now evidence in a homicide and we can't let mama touch the body and we have to restrain her at the same time counsel her while keeping up our guard against other possible shooters in the crowd. The only thing worse than that was handling a "dead child" call. Mom and dad wake up for the 6 a.m. feeding and their precious six-month old is cold, bluish, and nonresponsive. He is dead. All dead-child calls go to the police to investigate and make sure no foul play has occurred. Mom and sometimes dad are crying on your shoulder screaming "Why? Why?" Everyone has their personal views on the subject but now is not the time to postulate or hypothesize. At the same time, we cannot rule out mom or dad as a suspect until the baby is cleared by the coroner. So while you want to empathize with the parents, you don't want to get sucked in to emotional cognitive dissonance. I would say that these are the worst calls, but then I remember one night on patrol I watched a small aircraft crash on the high tension wires just two hundred feet in front of me and slam to the ground. I tried to get them out but watched in horror as they got burned alive. Their screams will forever haunt me. So will the smell of burned flesh.

In November of 1989, just a month after my partner had been severely wounded and partially paralyzed by a bullet, I was still assigned to the anti-gang unit at 77th Division. I was working the 6 p.m. to 2 a.m. shift. This was before we went to the 3/12 compressed work schedule. I honestly do not remember how the shift went except for the fact that I got off on time since I didn't work overtime. I had moved to Los Angeles in September of 1988 at God's direction. I had crashed my motorcycle way up in the Maritime providences of Eastern Canada and was left in a ditch paralyzed from the waist down. This was about six weeks before I was to start the LAPD academy, September 12, 1988. I only had about two weeks' notice to travel the three thousand miles to a state in which I knew nobody and had no support. I had an old 1978 Ford LTD that was burning more oil than gas. There was no way I could drive in three thousand miles and risk blowing an engine in Nebraska somewhere. So I flew out to Los Angeles about four days before the police academy started with just the clothes on my back. About two weeks into the academy, I purchased a 1987 Kawasaki Ninja motorcycle from another recruit. This is how I got back and forth to work. I didn't own a car yet.

Looking back on it, there are several clues that should have caught my attention. When I first left 77th Police Station at about 2:30 a.m. my mind was focused on my partner and the things that had transpired a month earlier during the shooting. Normally I don't leave my guard down. I am always running scenarios in my mind—the "what if" syndromes. What if I am taking a shower when a bad guy kicks in my door? So I kept a gun in the bathroom. What if I am sleeping I wake up with someone standing over me? So I kept a gun under the pillow. I used to have this recurring dream that I was kidnapped at gunpoint, handcuffed, driven to the ocean, and tossed off the end of a pier in deep water. I would gasp for air and struggle as I helplessly sunk to the bottom. I hated being out of control. In my job working some of the most hostile neighborhoods in the most violent city in America, the key to my survival was to always be in control. This night I really wasn't in control, at least not mentally. 77th Station is adjacent to the freeway. To gain access to the 110 Harbor Freeway South was just a quick turn out of the station and then up the winding onramp. As I maneuvered onto the onramp, I remember seeing headlights suddenly come on from a van parked at the bottom of the on ramp. In Los Angeles, it is not uncommon to have a little parking lot underneath freeway off and on ramps for Department of Transportation or freeway construction workers to park their vehicles or to store traffic cones, traffic signs, and other traffic related paraphernalia. I didn't think anything of it. Given the proximity to the station, time of night, and previous intelligence on ambushes, I should have seen a red flag. The second red flag should have registered as a clue but also fell on deaf ears, or mind if you will. As soon as I got on the 110 Freeway South and was about three miles down range near El Segundo boulevard off ramp, I suddenly saw bright lights come up behind me extremely fast and close. At the last second, I made a quick jerky move of the handle bars and quickly switched lanes as the van drove past me at about 80 mph.

I thought to myself that this must be a drunk who didn't see me. Instead of taking caution and using the counter surveillance skills I had learned, I just kept going straight as the van passed me, slowed a bit, and then suddenly leaped over into my lane and hit the brakes hard. I didn't have time to stop and rear-ended the van, sending me crashing down to the unforgiving pavement and into a spark filled slide at 70 mph. This was in 1989, several years before California passed the mandatory helmet law for motorcycles. All I had on was a pair of lightly tinted shades, vinyl sweats, and a T-shirt.

I remember going down and sliding on the pavement. Memories flooded my mind of me growing up back in New England sliding down a snowy hillside or ice skating full-speed racing my friends around the frozen pond in my backyard and then tripping and sliding on my stomach for a good thirty feet. Then I caught on fire. The gasoline had spilled from the motorcycle and was ignited by the stream of sparks dancing all around me. I was still sliding southbound on the freeway as sparks silhouetted me in the darkness, flesh being stripped from my body when I started to kick the motorcycle away. I wanted to get away from the source of the fire and heat although the pavement was doing a pretty good job inflicting friction burns. I was quickly heading toward the guardrail in the fast lane. Suddenly, my head struck the guardrail and I fell into a semi-conscious state. I stopped sliding and remember kind of lying there probably in shock because the pain hadn't settled in yet. It was foggy and very dark. I saw the van pull over to what I suddenly came to realize was a *coup de grace*. They were going to finish me off and shoot me in the head. I didn't have my weapon. This was back in the days when we were issued 38 Smith & Wesson revolvers. If you carried and off-duty weapon at all it was a two-inch five-shot revolver. My duty weapon was back in my locker along with my back up weapon and my off-duty weapon was at my apartment in Redondo Beach. I silently started to pray to the Lord because I was unarmed, semi-conscious, and unable to move. There were no other automobiles on the freeway and the fog gave natural cover to the individuals in the van. All of a sudden, I saw some headlights pierce through the fog and heard the sound of an engine slowing down. I looked back to see a passenger car slowing down and pulling over to the break down lane. I then swung my head back around to see where my would-be executers where. Two males with hoodies had started to make their way across the freeway toward me. When they saw a vehicle approaching and stopping, they quickly got back into their van and fled the scene southbound down the 110 freeway. Fading in and out of consciousness, I saw a white or Hispanic man come toward me on foot. I didn't recognize him but he was an off-duty gang officer from South Bureau CRASH (Community Resources Against Street Hoodlums). He asked me if I was okay and he said he was an off-duty officer. I told him that I was hurt and I suspected that the guys who had just left in the van were trying to kill me. He helped me to my feet and across the open freeway. Thank God no other traffic came barreling down on us. At almost three in the morning and in heavy fog no one would have been able to stop for a couple of pedestrians slowly limping across the freeway. Experience also told me that this was the time of evening/morning in which the freeway was full of drunk drivers. The officer let me lay down in the back of his car and drove me to Harbor General Hospital in the city of Carson about five miles away.

I don't really remember the ride to the hospital or even being taken into the emergency room. What I do remember was lots of pain. My plastic Adidas sweats had melted from the friction of the freeway surface as I slid along the pavement at 60 mph. As my skin became shredded and was removed by the friction, the black dye from the sweats tattooed my legs. Because there was no skin left, the dye acted like ink and was absorbed or burnt into my raw and bleeding flesh. I had second degree burns on about thirty percent of my body. My legs, arms, and some of my back were all void of skin and open wounds. The nurses explained to me that they needed to use surgical scrubs with iodine to remove dead and peeled away flesh and to scrub the black dye from my open wounds to prevent infection and black pigmentation or tattooing of my body. I am not sure why they didn't use anesthesia but I wish they had. I screamed in pain as they started to scrub all of my open wounds with iodine that stung and the rigid bristles of the brushes that felt like a brillo pad was being rubbed up and down on my skin.

After a little while, my watch commander, Sgt. Miller showed up at the hospital. We briefly talked but he could see I was in extreme pain so he kept the questions to a minimum. An attempted murder of a police officer is a serious thing. Especially when a certain group of gangs had declared they were going to "get" a gang cop. Was this retaliation for the shooting a month before? Suddenly, in walked the California Highway Patrol. I had very little contact with them in my first year in the field but their reputation proceeded them. They were not well-respected by law enforcement because their primary duty was traffic flow and violations of the state's freeway system. We called them "Triple A with gun." I then realized that they probably came upon my broken and burnt motorcycle that I left lying across the diamond lane of the 110 freeway. It wouldn't be too hard to figure someone involved and a motorcycle accident would go or be brought to the nearest hospital. My license plates were confidential so they would have, in the alternative, contacted my watch commander to get my information. My watch commander informed them that I may have been a victim of attempted murder and their response was to write me a citation for expired insurance. I had inadvertently let my motorcycle insurance lapse for a few weeks and it expired. Thankfully, a few months later, a sympathetic judge would dismiss the violation. When I look back on that incident, I think God must have sent the gang officer at exactly the right time. Timing is always key with God. Sometimes He waits until the last minute to give us that job we so desperately need or provide the rent a day before eviction. His timing is not always our timing but His timing is perfect.

A Christian Terrorist?

+ ✦ ✦ ✦ ✦ +

O n September 22, 1992, I was working patrol assigned to the LAPD Pacific Division. I received a radio call of a man with a gun and explosives on the seventh floor of the LAX Hyatt Hotel. I didn't know it at the time but I was about to have a chance encounter with the infamous domestic terrorist known as Rainbow Man. If you are over thirty-five years old, you might remember a very strange and flamboyant character that used to show up in some of the most famous sporting events in a giant rainbow wig and clown outfit sporting a John 3:16 sign. He would show up at the World Series, the Super Bowl etc. Cameras would always zoom in on him as it would offer amusement and a cheap shot at those who hold Christianity in contempt. Turns out that one day, he thought the world was going to end and apparently needed to get his message out to the public. Why wait for a sporting event when you can take hostages and use explosives to get your message across? As I got off the elevator, he had just taken a maid hostage at gunpoint who was cleaning a bathroom in a room on the seventh floor. We started setting up a perimeter on the escape route like stairwells and elevators, and set up a shooting gallery in the hallway in case he was stupid enough to stick his head out the door so we could separate it from his body. I had brought my slug shotgun to the fight which at the time was the most powerful weapon we patrol officers had. Later, after the North Hollywood shooting, we would receive AR 15s which was nicknamed the LAPD Urban Assault Rifle.

We established a line of communication from the lobby up to his room and those who specialize in crisis negotiation were speaking with him. Those officers that were with me in that hallway as well as myself were solely focused on the hotel room door. It was his only avenue of escape because he was not going to jump out of a seventh-story window. One rule of hostage negotiation is that you never let the suspect leave the location with a hostage. He wasn't going to get past us with a hostage. It is not like the movies or cop shows on television. You never let a bad guy leave an area once contained with a hostage. Usually a supervisor will designate someone to be the designated shooter and draw an imaginary line of demarcation as a boundary. The suspect was not allowed to go past the boundary and if he did he would be shot. Our fatal flaw in our plan was that we knew that he had already barricaded himself in the room with the hostage. We thought we had heard him barricade himself and the hostage into the room so he wasn't coming out that way any time soon. We also knew that being on the seventh floor, he wasn't going to be able to escape out the window. One thing he did have was a clear shot at planes landing at LAX Airport. I am not sure, given the distance, how effective a small caliber weapon could be but it was enough to start thinking about re-routing air traffic at LAX. We also didn't know that he had a background as an amateur chemist. The information I had at the time of the incident was that besides being armed, he may have explosives and he had threatened to blow up the building. So as I was perched behind a door jam in the hallway outside the hotel room and about twenty feet down the hallway, I started to think that at any minute we could all be blown up. After a long period of waiting, he acted.

All of a sudden, the door to the hotel room that led out to the hallway opened ajar. Out came a clear class jar which looked like a mayonnaise jar. I can't quite remember if it hit the wall first and then the floor or just the floor, but what I do remember is it shattering and a colorless, semi-odorless vapor began to emanate from the jar and fill the air. No one had a gas mask. It wouldn't be until after the events of 9/11 did we start carrying them around with us in our war bags in the trunk of the police car. The hallway was long and rectangular with no windows to open and no real cover to speak of. I was about the third officer furthest away from the vapor and I watched as it began to cause reactions in one officer closest to it and then the other. I could see they were a little agitated, not knowing if this was harmless or sarin or ricin or some other kind of noxious and toxic gas. The first officer started to rub his eyes and took out a handkerchief and tried to cover his face while maintaining his focus on the doorway where the gas had just been tossed from. No one knew if this was a prelude to a further attack. Again, information had also come out that Rainbow Man had enough explosives to blow up the building. I think this was the worst part—standing there the entire time as the seconds turned into minutes and minutes eventually turned into hours not knowing if you were going to live or die. The uncertainty of it was the worst. LAPD officers face down death almost every day. In fact, we live for it. Everyone responds to a shooting-in-progress or a vehicle chase in-progress because we want that adrenaline rush and the thrill of facing death. It is not maniacal but it almost makes up for the endless paper work.

I thought for sure that when we communicated to the command post that we were now being exposed to possible poisonous gas and in fact, inhaling it, they would have us evacuate or at least retreat to the ends of the hallway and in the stairwells were we could be treated by paramedics and still keep an eye on the door and prevent escape of Rainbow Man and the hostage. Instead, we were given orders to hold our positions and tough it out until SWAT relieved us. To the layman, this probably seems innocuous. We see on television how a couple of police officers or detectives get pinned down by gunfire and SWAT responds in a matter of minutes. Not so in real life. I cannot tell you how many times I have been on SWAT call outs and had to wait hours for them to respond. One time I was pinned down by gunfire in the backyard of a residence when the owner decided to use me and my partner for target practice. The only cover was a small, wooden boat that had been tipped on its side. It was more concealment than cover but it was better than nothing. After a long time, SWAT finally arrived on the scene and I knew it because it came over the radio. I expected them to make their way to me and my partner to get us out any minute. However, it was another hour before they got to us. You see, SWAT takes their time. They often have to respond from the farthest parts of the city or from being off-duty. When they do finally get to the scene, they plan. I have seen them take over an hour to plan a mission once on scene. Out comes the brown butcher paper on the hood of a police car and diagrams begin to be drawn as intelligence is gathered. I am in no way disparaging or defaming LAPD SWAT guys. They are the best. I was deeply saddened when my fellow brother in Christ and former teammate on the LAPD football team Randy Simmons was killed. He was a SWAT team leader. The point I am making is that people are misguided because of the fact that modern culture gets its information on police activities and functions from television and the movies.

Meanwhile, on the seventh floor, police officers were suffering. Patrol officers, including me, were throwing up, struggling to keep their vision, and having difficulty breathing as we were all now being exposed to this gas. I can't tell you how much longer it was before SWAT finally relieved us. It seemed like hours. Eventually, SWAT relieved us (at least they had the good sense to have gas masks). They made entry and were able to actually take the suspect (Rainbow Man) in custody and rescue the hostage without killing anyone. This is rare when forced entry is made in a hostage situation and no one is killed. Later, during the prosecution phase, Rainbow Man was offered twenty-five years in federal prison as part of a plea deal with the United States Attorney's Office. He refused to plea and insisted on acting as his own attorney and instead received three consecutive life terms in prison from the jury. I thank God for getting me out of there alive, albeit not undamaged.

The sad part is that many officers were exposed to this chemical grenade or homemade bomb that Rainbow Man had thrown at us. Some officers experienced loss of vision, lung irritation, and skin damage. Even sadder is that the City of Los Angeles would not reveal to the officers exposed to this chemical what was in this make-shift grenade. We finally had to threaten to bring a lawsuit before we were told it contained a chemical called butyl mercaptan. OSHA categorizes butyl mercaptan as a hazardous substance. Some of the immediate effects of being exposed to this chemical are irritation to the skin, eyes, nose, throat, and lungs. Long-term effects are: cancer, lung damage, bronchitis, eye damage. These side effects can last for months or even years. We spent hours breathing that stuff in. The protocol for exposure to butyl mercaptan is immediate medical attention and treatment. Officers like myself that were exposed had to wait weeks and threaten a lawsuit before we were even told what it was. I am convinced that it was the source of my persistent annual pneumonia and permanent loss of vision in my left eye. I was however, nominated for the Medal of Valor, which is the highest award given in law enforcement. However, I ended up being awarded the Police Medal which is LAPD's second highest award and I was inducted into the American Police Hall of Fame and given the Silver Star for bravery.

Career Taking Off

◆◆◆◆◆

B y the summer of 1994, my entire life was getting ready to take off. I had been volunteering in the ministry for about four years now and was being disciple and growing in the faith. I was ministering to a few officers at Pacific Division of LAPD and sharing the word. I was getting married to the love of my life who I had actually met on the job. She was the victim of a burglary of which I responded to. I had been with LAPD now for six years and my career, while not perfect, had been good. I was allowed to work specialized details on probation because of my prior law enforcement experience. I was assigned to several specialized units including gangs, Oakwood Task Force and the Venice Beach Detail. I was about to be published on the sergeant's promotion list which would have made one of the youngest sergeants (tenure wise) in the LAPD at that time. I had also just earned my first master's degree, one of seven college degrees I would eventually earn. Soon, I would start teaching college part-time as a criminal justice professor. I had received numerous commendations and the Police Star and the Police Medal for bravery. Everything I always wanted was now happening or in sight. However, within a year everything would change and God would challenge me and take away just about every covetous thing in my life. Much like the freshly liberated Hebrews that took forty years to make an eleven-day journey to the Promised Land, I would spend the next eighteen years in the proverbial desert. However, they would be spiritually eventful years.

Around the spring of 1995, I was assigned to the Venice Beach Detail. This was quite a change from working South Central Los

Angeles with all of its gangs, urban blight, and unrest. Many officers wanted to work the beach detail for several reasons. First, you were getting paid to drive a police car, ride a bicycle, or walk up and down the boardwalk and beach area. The Venice Beach detail was considered to be a specialized assignment because as foot beat officers, we didn't have to carry a call load. Those patrol officers assigned to an "A" car or patrol beat were responsible for handling radio traffic, calls for service, citizen flag downs, and other incidences for their assigned area. It wasn't uncommon to get twenty-five radio calls for service in a twelve hour shift. This could be everything from rapes to robberies to vehicle break-ins to family disputes. You would spend the entire shift running from call to call to call, often not even enough time to eat. It wasn't uncommon to have to drive twenty miles from one call to the next if you had to go into another division because they were busy. Not so with a specialized unit like the Venice Beach detail. You didn't have to handle radio calls for service so in essence, you got to create your own police work. Another reason why it was such a popular detail was the overtime. There was plenty of cash overtime to go around in a department that didn't give out much. Most overtime was CTO or time compensation. Those on the detail also could wear shorts as part of their uniform and drive four-runners and quads. The hours were great as well. Although in the summer time, they ran a night shift, most beach detail officers worked the midday shift from 10 a.m. until 6 p.m. This allowed you to sleep in during the mornings or workout and still get home at a good time and miss most of the rush hour traffic. I would be negligent to leave out one of the primary reasons many officers want to work the beach detail and that would be the hundreds of thousands of tourists (insert imagination here) that come to Venice Beach making it the second largest tourist attraction in California. Getting free memberships at Gold's Gym Venice and watching them film television shows like *Bay Watch* or *Pacific Blue* was also a perk.

The Los Angeles Police Department's Pacific Division encompassed two sub-stations in which one is the aforementioned Venice Beach Station and one is at Los Angeles International Airport. The brief history with Pacific Division which became known to me since I arrived there in July of 1990 was that it was a haven for lesbian police officers. I was a little naive when it came to gay and lesbian issues, having come from a small town in New England and never knowing a gay or lesbian individual. I had nothing against them. I was just ignorant much like I was ignorant of African-American people because of lack of exposure to their culture growing up. When I arrived at Pacific Division, there was a lesbian LAPD captain-in-charge of the division. It was rumored that she had an ongoing lesbian relationship with a Los Angeles City councilwoman who was a self-admitted lesbian. Whether this was true or not, it seemed to give credibility to the fact that this female captain systematically recruited lesbian offices to work at Pacific Division under her command from all over the city. Beginning in 1991, many were transferred in to Pacific Division from various other divisions around the City. Within a few years, their number grew enough and they sensed that this captain had their backs that some of them became very brazen. Complaints were made by heterosexual female offices that they felt they were being discriminated against. Reports of being leered at in the locker room and even groped in the showers began to emerge. Having worked there during this time, I can tell you from personal experience and from speaking with many of the young female police officers there that they felt intimidated and that they felt if they reported these violations it would result in them getting in trouble but not the lesbian officers. Eventually, as part of an administrative settlement, two female locker rooms were created—one upstairs and one downstairs. It still remains this way although most officers modernly don't know the history.

Another problem that developed within the ranks of the lesbian officers was that some of them began having intimate relations with each other, even among supervisors and subordinates which is forbidden. Domestic violence also started occurring. It wasn't that uncommon for one of them to come to work with a black eye. Everyone knew what was going on but were afraid to say anything out of fear of retaliation from the captain and LAPD management which was heavily recruiting in the gay and lesbian community. The case of Officer Angela Sheppard highlights this. Officer Sheppard had been involved with another female officer, Officer Loomis, in a lesbian relationship for some time. I knew both officers and had no problems with either one of them. On February 19, 1995, the two got into a late-night argument over the phone. Sheppard said she was coming over to discuss their disagreement. She arrived about an hour later with her service pistol in her hand and got into a fight with Loomis on the front porch. After the fight, a restraining order was issued against Officer Sheppard. The Police Department also began an investigation. On June 2, 1995, Sheppard was told she would have to appear at an LAPD discipline hearing called a Board of Rights about the complaint. That day, she returned to Loomis' house. She knocked on the door, got no response, then walked around the side and broke in through a sliding glass door. Meanwhile, Loomis had gone into her bedroom, picked up her semiautomatic pistol and called police. Sheppard confronted her in the bedroom, shouted at her, and pushed her in the chest. Sheppard saw Loomis' gun and said, "What are you going to do, shoot me?" Then Sheppard saw the phone and yelled, "Who's on the phone? You better not call anyone or I'm going to kill you." She then hit Loomis on the head and back, according to the investigation. Loomis pointed the gun at Sheppard and fired a warning shot into the bed. Shepard said, "I'm going to kill you; you're dead," before she left the room. According to the investigation, Loomis ran outside, where a sheriff's deputy had just arrived. The deputy arrested Sheppard and booked her at the Walnut Sheriff's station. In 2001, Officer Sheppard would murder her then-girlfriend, former USC basketball star Audrey Gomez and be sentenced to fifteen years to life in prison. It is hard to imagine this happening as I had worked with Officer Sheppard and she was always nice to me and professional.

One thing that needs to be highlighted here is the double standard. I stood by and watched male officers get suspended and even terminated for much less than what Officer Shepard did and much quicker as well. It wasn't just officer Sheppard but there was a lot of inter-departmental sexual relations going on at Pacific Division among the lesbian officers and everyone knew it. There was a lot of domestic violence going on within those relationships as well.

Management turned a blind eye to it because they put diversity ahead of ethical considerations. Everyone in Pacific Division, including the command staff, knew what was going on but looked the other way out of fear of reprisal. It wasn't just Pacific Division. LAPD had a huge push to recruit gay and lesbian officers but especially female lesbians. The climate was created to encourage apathy when it came to holding lesbian officers accountable which created a de facto double standard. It wasn't just Sheppard either. It seemed to me to be pandemic. In fact, as I mentioned, the command at Pacific Division even created a separate female locker room for lesbian officers. There is a female locker room upstairs and a female locker room down stairs—one for lesbians and one for heterosexual female officers. This was not done so much for the lesbian officers than to placate the complaints of being groped and sexually harassed by the straight female officers. The widespread double standard and disparate treatment of officers in the face of growing prima facie evidence of its existence militated against the social and political narrative of the LAPD agenda. It was an inconvenient truth that would eventually align its sights on me.

By summer of 1995, we had a new female captain take over patrol at Pacific Division. She was not, as far as I know, a lesbian, however she was a staunch feminists and a very political savvy individual. She wasn't at Pacific Division very long when the whole lesbian event was boiling over. Complaints were being filed by heterosexual female officers, some of the more ardent and aggressive lesbian officers were being administratively transferred all over the city quietly. I had just got transferred to the Venice Beach detail from Pacific Division Patrol and as I said before, it was not easy to get on because it was a coveted position for all the reasons I outlined previously. So when I was transferred to the beach detail in May of 1995, I was very happy. I had earned it. I think that the new captain felt obligated mainly out of political concern and nepotism to take care of the lesbian officers and so in an effort to take care of them and in a way shepherd them, transferred a bunch of them over to the Venice Beach Detail where I was now assigned. Many of these officers had not earned the right to be chosen to the beach detail and hadn't done their time and jumped over other more senior officers and officers who had waited a long time to get to the Venice Beach Detail.

In the month of May of each year, tourism in and around Venice Beach picks up. This normally causes a transfer to Venice Beach Detail of about a dozen more police officers to handle the summer crowds and associated problems that comes with this yearly event. During an average Saturday in December on Venice Beach, we might get five hundred to five thousand visitors, depending on the weather. During an average Saturday in July, we would get over one hundred thousand visitors. During the winter time, the beach detail would carry only about six to eight police officers and run mainly a midday shift. During the summer time, the ranks would swell up to twenty police officers and would be embellished on weekends by over time units. During the peak of Venice Beach which was from about 1991 to about 1998, we would have up to a total of fifty police officers included on foot, on bike, on motorcycle, on horseback, and in cars on any given summer weekend. A second shift was added during this time which as a night shift from 6:00 p.m. until 2:00 a.m. There were always sign-up sheets for overtime and again, it was coveted because LAPD did not give out a lot of cash overtime and not everyone on the beach detail got it. One of the first things that I began to notice was that several of the lesbian officers were falsifying their overtime reports and thus stealing. I won't get into their exact scheme but it was well known. They also were given special treatment and given overtime over other more experienced and senior officers. This created some resentment but the supervisor in charge of the beach detail wouldn't say anything. I could tell he was scared. Anytime I would broach the subject with him by dropping innuendos or colloquiums on the topic, he would get uneasy and quickly change the subject.

Another issue that was going on was that some of these lesbian officers were having sex on duty. Especially during the week days when things are slow, this became evident. One of the officers had a crash pad on Abbot-Kinney Boulevard which was only about three blocks from the beach. Many of these beach officers were dating and having relationships in common. I was actually asked several times by a couple of them if I was interested in a *ménage à trois*. I found it rather paradoxical that a lot of lesbian officers liked to share their girlfriends with other guys. I found myself in a rather awkward position. I was pretty open about my faith and my Christianity. At the same time, I discovered that there were also a lot of LAPD officers that called themselves Christians but were either Chinos (Christians in Name Only) or CEO's (Christmas and Easter-Only believers). So I understood why that despite my openness about my faith they would still ask me. In the flesh, a threesome with two young girls is a lot of men's fantasy. Not me. So I had to politely refuse their request without offending them.

By the time July of 1995 came around, I was really sick and tired of the preferential treatment, stealing, and other nefarious things being done with impunity by these officers. I made a decision that would start a chain of events so cruel, so corrupt, so underhanded, that it would last the next eighteen years and almost take my life. The sergeant in charge of the Venice Beach Detail was the quintessential don't-rock-the-boat supervisor. I went to him and explained that he needed to do something about the corruption going on which everyone knew about but looked the other way. Under the Los Angeles Police Department policy and under most law enforcement code of ethics, it is mandatory that any employee, sworn or civilian, report misconduct once they become cognizant of it. You would think that when I came forward with this information, which was really nothing new, that he would be attentive to take my statement and investigate as well as report it up the chain of command. Instead, I was met with a well-meaning but ominous warning. The sergeant warned me, "If I make a complaint on this, it is going to go to the Captain. This could end your career." This sergeant was well aware of the history of these lesbian officers and the protection afforded them by the Pacific Division Command Staff. I was told that it even involved certain people in the Police Commission and the City Council. I told him that I was certain that I wanted to go through with it so he took my statement. It took just two days before I was called into the captain's office. I reaffirmed to her after given the chance to retract my allegations what I knew to be true.

The only way to cover wrong doing within the department when there is invidious evidence of misconduct and corruption is to terminate or to discredit that person so they just seem like a disgruntled employee or former employee. We saw what happened with Officer Christopher Dorner and his revenge killings. No one can condone what he did. However, few people realize that it started out much like the details of my demise—reporting an incident of misconduct and then being retaliated for it. No good deed goes unpunished. Once they discredit you, then every attempt by that individual down the road to legitimately seek justice of recompense for being wronged by the LAPD administration, as we saw in the Christopher Dorner case, would be structured to look like a disgraced employee trying to frame himself as a whistle blower and good-doer only to cover their ineptitude. This is what happened to me within a few weeks of reporting this gross misconduct. The next thing I know, I was the subject of a theft complaint. The Venice Beach Bike Detail to which I was assigned had a contract with the City of Los Angeles to furnish parts and fix city bicycles. I had gone to a city-approved and licensed bicycle dealer to obtain some mandatory equipment for the job. I was originally sent there several months previously at the behest of one of these lesbian officers for the first time. She told me that since I was new to the bike unit, that she was showing me how things worked. She said I would need a bicycle helmet and gloves per department policy. She then had me call the LAPD Supply Division and get a purchase order number (PPO). The number was then given to the bicycle store owner so they could bill the city for the parts or maintenance work. So I did. Turns out that the city contract with the bicycle company only covered repairs and bicycle parts but not accessories. My helmet and gloves were considered accessories even though the department required them to work the bicycle detail.

This lesbian officer went back to that same store a few weeks later right after I had filed my complaint against her and the other co-conspirators. The owner of the store said to her (I found out later in the investigation) "Tell Brooks that the city is denying his PPO and that when he gets a chance to come down and pay me. No rush." Obviously there was either a misunderstanding by the city or by the owner but all I did was what I was told by this officer as the new guy on the block. Well she didn't waste any time. Instead of coming to me as requested by the owner, she went right to the captain that was out to get me. She twisted it or they both twisted the facts to make it look like I was willfully and purposefully stealing from this shop owner. Sure enough, within a few days, I was served with a complaint alleging theft which they knew was the kiss of death for any officer's career if sustained. Since I had also just came out very high on the sergeant's promotion list and would very assuredly promote to sergeant within a year, they also saw a chance to stop me from promoting to add insult to injury. I was immediately taken off the Beach Detail, one in which I had worked very hard to get on, and placed on the front desk of Pacific Station. This may not sound so bad but working the front desk at one of the twenty geographical LAPD divisions is the worse job there is. The lobby is constantly full of people reporting everything from burglaries of their homes, cars, bicycles to assault and batteries, robberies, stolen cars, missing persons and so on. Also, the phones don't ever stop ringing as people continuously call the front desk for everything from neighbor disputes to vandalisms to family squabbles. It was twelve hours of continuous stress, noise, and shouting and sometimes fighting. People would run into the station and collapse on the lobby floor from being stabbed. On Fridays when weekend court ordered child custodial occurred, it was often chaotic. The court's got smart and decided to start having court ordered custody exchange of minor children in common at the lobby of the local police station. The wisdom was that decent folks wouldn't be foolish enough to start trouble in the police station. Well as soon as one parent dropped off the kid(s) and left, the other parent would march the child to the officer at the front desk and show a scratch on the child and demand a child abuse report just to get back at the other parent for some petty issue. The most violent incidences happen when a custodial drop off occurs and one of the parents shows up with a new boyfriend or girlfriend. The thought of someone else raising their kid or perhaps having relationship with their former spouse is enough to cause tempers to erupt. I once saw a man after dropping of his two kids to his ex-wife who was accompanied by her new lover, run out of the police station and across the police parking lot and jump onto the hood of the ex-spouses car as it was driving away. Emotions can run extremely high at the front desk. It kind of reminds me of some scenes from that television show called *Hardcore Pawn*. Crazy people are not solely indigenous to Detroit however.

I would spend the next couple of years working the desk. As I said, it was very stressful and LAPD command staff new it was. I once saw a very good friend of mine who was a former partner, Christian, and boxer like me have a heart attack from the stress and go off in an ambulance. He collapsed at the front desk from the stress the position was putting on him. He, like me, had fallen out of favor with Pacific Division Command and was being punished despite the fact that LAPD policy is that the desk assignment cannot be used as a form of punishment. As soon as he was medically cleared to come back to work, they put him right back to the front desk despite his doctor's orders to be put in a non-stressful work environment. He was like me—persona non-grata. He had high-blood pressure which kept him from working the field which management interpreted as lazy. Every time he called in sick, they would harass him by sending a supervisor to his house for a "sick check." I also saw one officer punch another police officer in the face at the front desk. This particular officer had recently caught his wife cheating on him in his own bed with another woman. He was seeing a psychologist and counselor and renting a room. The worst place they could put him was at the front desk which, not to over exaggerate, but is probably the most stressful job on the department maybe outside of the bomb squad. Another officer was working the front desk with him that was a little cocky and interpreted the other officers slow to answer the phone as slothfulness. He kept mouthing off to the officer who was understandably consumed mentally and emotionally with his personal life. Suddenly, the officer snapped and punched the officer in the side of the head. A little shoving match ensued but it was broken up quickly. This officer was terminated for throwing the punch despite LAPD doing everything to set up that reaction but cocking his fist back. When I was in law school, they use to call it the "but for test." In negligence, you would have to prove that "but for" the actions of the defendant the plaintiff never would have gotten hurt. Nothing could be truer in the instant case.

As I mentioned before, I had recently came out very high on the published sergeant's list and was expecting to promote to sergeant within about a year. It wasn't unusual for four hundred police officers and detectives to take the LAPD sergeant's exam which was given every two years and was good for two years of eligibility. It is a two-part exam consisting of a written exam and an oral interview panel. That ends up being about twenty "bands" or rankings from one hundred score on down to seventy-five. Only the top ten bands are published city-wide and these people are almost guaranteed to make sergeant unless a promotional freeze occurs or, drum roll please, a serious complaint of misconduct is alleged. I had made the top ten bands and so my name was published city-wide. All I had to do to make sergeant was to stay out of trouble which I had managed to do for most of my career up until that point. Everything was in place. I had just earned my first master's degree, I had a relatively clean complaint record, had worked a few specialized assignments, and had received the Police Star and the Police Medal for bravery and heroism.

The Boards

+ + + + + +

The Los Angeles Police Department use to have what could be easily be construed as a kangaroo court called the Board of Inquiry (BOI). Think of Captain Queeg in the *Caine Mutiny*. An undiagnosed obsessive compulsive captain of a ship on a mission to find out who took the missing strawberries that he was determined to find out despite all of the primae facia evidence to the contrary. This is how these boards of inquiries use to go. I say used to because thanks to the Gregson Brown lawsuit of which I was a part of, these hearings are now illegal because they lacked any type of due process and evidentiary rules. About a month before I was due to promote to sergeant and my complaint of theft of the bicycle accessories was still being investigated, I was ordered to a Board of Inquiry. Unlike the LAPD Board of Rights which are based on administrative laws and rules of evidence, the BOI's have no rules. Just three command staff officers that sit there and listen to a bunch of ringers who are brought in for the sole purpose of defaming the individual as rationale for not promoting you. Many of these command staff officers have been accused of such crimes as sex crimes, child molestation, drunk driving, and other acts of stupidity which are much worse than the allegations being adjudicated by the poor soul sitting at the defendant's table. Well, in my hearing, the department advocate was a female sergeant who was one of the most ardent lesbians on the department and use to work Pacific Division and knew I was a Christian. During the entire process, you could tell she had contempt for me. During my closing statement, I wasn't really sure what to say because I know I didn't do anything wrong so I said, "I am a Christian, I wouldn't do such a thing as steal." Right when I said this, I looked at this sergeant and when she heard those words come out of my mouth, you could tell she wanted to scream something derogatory. She looked at the chair of the board and rolled her eyes at him and he in turn rolled his eyes. It was at that point I knew that they were never going to promote me.

Unlike Boards of Rights, the decision to recommend punitive action including promotions or to deny it was not concurrent with the trial but came weeks later after being taken under submission. To no one's surprise including mine, I was denied the opportunity to promote to sergeant and it wouldn't be the last time. These boards were really a violation of any type of due processes and property rights which explains why they are now banned. Now one thing that I learned from going through an eighteen-year ordeal and having put myself through law school is that there is always an appeal mechanism. In my case, the equitable remedy was to go across the street and file a writ of mandamus in Los Angeles Superior Court. These are a special type of writ that if the judge agrees with the petitioner, can overturn the Board's decision if it can be proven there was a manifest abuse of discretion by the Board of Inquiry or a Board of Rights. One thing that is needed however, are the transcripts of the hearing. When an appeal is filed, whether criminally, civilly, or administratively, judges need to read the transcripts. When an appeal brief is written (and I have written many) allegations of wrongful conduct during the hearing must be pointed out by referring to the transcripts of the hearing and the page and line of the transcript. When I sat there during the Board of Inquiry, I was a percipient witness to the fact that not only was there a court stenographer there diligently taking notes and recording the entire trial but that it was also being tape recorded by a Los Angeles Police Department's Advocate (Administrative Prosecutor) who would pause from time to time to change the tape or turn it over (this is before digital recorders). By administrative rule, I had to wait the mandatory ninety days before subpoenaing the transcripts and recordings but mainly the transcripts. In order to file a writ of mandamus, you had to provide the judge with the transcripts of the trial. Of course, you would write an appellate brief and cite case law but mainly in your legal brief, you point the judge to errors in the law, procedure, or failure to follow proper procedure during the trial by putting down the transcript pages next to your argument. In short, you could not file a successful writ and have your LAPD hearing overturned if you didn't have the transcripts which themselves cost about $5,000 apiece. Of course the LAPD knew full well that if I didn't have the hearing transcripts, I couldn't win my appeal. So their decided upon tactic would be to simply "lose" the transcripts. I kid you not.

As an example of how dirty and how corrupt and with how much disdain they look at an employee that dares challenge their hegemony over the internal discipline system, I will explain what they did to me. After they ruled that I should no longer be in consideration for promotion to the rank of sergeant, a month goes by after the hearing takes place and I requested the transcripts as described in the Memorandum of Understanding and by law. Another month goes by and still nothing on the formal request in writing for the transcripts. My lawyer then sends an official demand to both the chair of the board, the captain of Wilshire Division, as well as to the City Attorney's Office for the transcripts. Soon after, I get a certified letter back in the mail from the captain of Wilshire Division and chairman of the Board of Inquiry. The letter states that he (the captain) is sorry but the Board of Inquiry that took place at his division and in which he was the chair of, seemed to have lost all evidence of the Board of Inquiry. The transcripts got lost and the tape recordings somehow got lost. Here is the best part which was the closing line of the letter: "Good luck in your future endeavors with the Los Angeles Police Department."

One thing that I did know was that the transcripts were completed by an outside professional court reporting agency who were contracted out by the Los Angeles Police Department. These were not LAPD employees and had direct control over the transcripts. The reason why transcripts are so expensive ($5,000 to $10,000) is that they must be certified as authentic representation of the trial because they are, in essence, evidence. I can understand how easily LAPD could purposely "lose" the tape recordings since they were in their dominion. However, the transcripts must have taken a concerted effort to make go away sort of like Hilary Clinton's emails. So this is a snap shot of how, for over a decade and one half, that LAPD management would eviscerate, retaliate and create a hostile work environment for any employee that they had a "gotcha" for or simply didn't like. You could study your butt off for two years, get a top score on the promotional written exam and the oral interview panel, and then when your name is about to be published and you are getting promoted to detective, sergeant or lieutenant for example, someone in management who doesn't like you can simply pull you into a Board of Inquiry. There, they can make up all the rules because there literally are none. At least for the Board of Rights, there is a procedural manual and you are working under administrative law with rules of evidence and procedure. The Boards of Inquiries was a joke. They were a set up from the beginning and a way for which if someone they don't like or, in my case, don't agree with my religious practice and challenge of their autonomy somehow slips through the system to stop them in their tracks. They know they can simply bring an officer in and berate them, belittle them, and defame them much like Caiaphas did to Christ in front of the Sanhedrin. They know there is nothing you can do. Even if they believe that you made a valid point or that their accusations are baseless and think you might have their decision overturned, they simply lose any and all evidence of the Board of Inquiry so that you cannot win. Much like Lois Learner and the Internal Revenue Scandal in which several years of exculpatory and incriminating emails simply disappeared on a crashed hard drive, the LAPD just does what it wants because there are no consequences for such an abuse of authority. Even if you somehow are successful at obtaining the transcripts of a Board of Rights or a Board of Inquiry, the odds of prevailing in a writ of mandamus are about ten to one against you. Thus, the administrative punitive system is almost infallible from a managerial point of point. These command staff members know that the chances of them getting caught retaliating against a subordinate are next to nothing. Even if you are successful in challenging them in a court of law, such as I have, they are never held accountable as they would in a private sector job. I remember hearing from the Los Angeles Police Protective League (Union) that Chief Bernard Parks alone cost the city taxpayers approximately forty million dollars ($40,000,000) in wrongful termination lawsuits but was never held accountable to taxpayers as none of LAPD management is regardless of how many laws and polices they have broken.

The Noose Tightens

◆ ◆ ◆ ◆ ◆ ◆

From 1996 to 1998, despite my outstanding personnel record and having my master's degree and over thirty commendations and awards, I was placed on the aforementioned front desk duty for further punishment. Also, during this time, I was the victim of five false personnel complaints against me. One of these led to a Board of Rights. I was accused of working off-duty without a work permit. The one thing about LAPD that many outsiders don't understand is that management wants to control every aspect of your life—on and off duty. So they require any police officer who wants to get a second part time job doing security or teaching or just about anything that doesn't involve an Alcohol Beverage Commission license, to submit an off-duty work permit application that has to be signed off on by your commanding officer as well as other higher ups. If they want to screw with you and hurt you financially then they would simply reject your application and give no reason why. You could grieve it through the formal grievance process which could take a year. I had had a work permit to work off-duty security at a local outdoor mall in Marian del Rey. I had had the permit for six years which I had re-applied for each year and it was renewed. Well, this same Captain, the one that has been after me now for three years since I reported misconducted going on at Venice Beach, knew I was testing for sergeant and detective again and she wanted to either get me fired or give me such a bad personnel record that no promotion board would give me a passing score. She had one of her cronies go into my file and destroy the work permit I had for that location doing security. She then sent a supervisor by the off-duty job who interrogated me in front of my subordinates about whether or not I had a work permit for the job. This Captain was hoping that I would say yes to the supervisor who had me on tape that I did in fact have a work permit on file so that she could then turn around and try to terminate me for lying to a supervisor. However, much to the surprise of the supervisor, after affirming I did have one on file and him retorting that he could not locate one in my file, I whipped out a copy of my work permit signed by him and by the captain. I also did it in front of five witnesses who worked for me. I was getting smarter toward their schemes.

The sergeant then fumbled for words and said "Well how do I know it's for real?" I wasn't stupid and had learned from past mistakes. Anywhere, I worked off-duty I made a copy of that permit and carried it on my on the work site. I thought that would be the end of it but of course not. The Captain knew that I was coming up for a promotional interview soon and that having an open and active complaint would be the kiss of death. You see, even a bogus complaint can stay in the system a long time. Under the California Peace Officers Bill of Rights, the law enforcement organization has a year to complete their administrative investigation. Once again, playing games with people's lives and careers they would use the system to hurt people. This was this captain's *modus operandus* which was simply a form of cognitive dissonance ideology that no officer or employee not of management caliber could challenge their draconian system of management and punishment. To do so was prima facie evidence of malfeasances. I would be subject to three other complaints filed against me during this time which was a premeditated plan to destroy my career, my good name and reputation, and to lay the foundation to terminate me by showing a long-pattern of misconduct and failure to learn from positive discipline.

Besides losing my promotion to sergeant and having to fend off five false complaints against me, I was victimized by yet another Board of Inquiry but this time for the rank of detective. It was the usual set up. As soon as I took the stand, it was one hostile inquisitional question after another staining my reputation and decision making ability. I knew it was a moot point to try to even rebut a lot of the allegations made against me. However, I had learned another thing about the discipline system and managerial philosophy of the LAPD. I realized that no matter how weak their case was against me and how strong of a defense I might have, I would never see justice inside the walls of any LAPD disciplinary board or promotional hearing. I started utilizing the philosophy of creating an appeal I would use to go to court with. In other words, I was no longer interested in trying to persuade a panel of three LAPD Command staff officers or in the case of a Board of Rights two command staff officers and one civilian that I was not guilty of the charges. Instead I focused on preparing a defense based on the rules of evidence, labor codes, administrative law, and the government codes that would persuade a judge or jury of my innocence. It was at this Board of Inquiry that I had now been through two Boards of Rights, two Boards of Inquiries, three law suits, three grievances and two writs of mandamus. All this in about three years. Four years earlier, I stood on the precipice of what many within the organization would consider a success. Because of my previous law enforcement experience, I was allowed to work specialized assignments while on probation; had worked several successive specialized assignments; had excellent ratings; was awarded numerous commendations including the second and third highest within LAPD—the Police Star and the Police Medal; I had just earned my first master's degree in Organizational Management and Leadership and was hired as an adjunct professor of criminal justice at a local public university. On a personal front, I had just gotten married to the woman of my dreams. She had owned a clothing store in Venice Beach, California that was burglarized. She called the police and I got the call and responded. We soon started dating, fell in love and have been married for over twenty-two years now. Who says crime doesn't pay? I became more than upset at what the LAPD was doing to me in response to making them aware of misconduct. I became apoplectic in nature. Consequently, my attitude took a gestalt shift from a defensive posture to one of offense.

I think one of the most difficult parts was trying to understand where God was in all this. After all, He called me three thousand miles from my home—the only real home I had known—to a very violent place in which I knew no one in the entire state or even west of the Mississippi River for that matter. He asked me to give up my very promising career with the Massachusetts State Police or the United States Marshals for which I was already interning. It reminds me of Jesus talking about the parable of the Sower and the Seed (Matthew 13:1-23). There are four different responses to the gospel in that parable. As we know from scripture, a farmer scattered seed which fell unto four different soils. Some seed fell on a path and the birds swiftly came and ate it; some fell on rocky soil and it became quickly withered because of the shallowness of roots and the soil and scorched sun withered it; others fell among thorns which eventually choked the seeds and; the fourth seed fell on good soil and produced good fruit and crop. To me, this tells me that three out of four individuals who give their life to Christ whether in an alter call or Harvest Festival or Crusade or whatever, will eventually fall away. Would this be me? I am not militating against those that argue the dogma of "Once saved, always saved." Rather more in alignment with what John says in that "They went out from us, but they did not really belong to us. For if they had belonged to us, they would have remained with us; but their going showed that none of them belonged to us" (John 2:19). I think a lot of people who call themselves Christians, especially Orthodox Christians and Roman Catholics, are not truly saved because they are not taught to enter into a living relationship with Jesus Christ and to become born again in which Jesus makes it very clear that this is the only way to become saved. Jesus replied, "Very truly I tell you, no one can see the kingdom of God unless they are born again" (John 3:3).

Just four years earlier as discussed, it seemed like I had everything I wanted. At least humanly speaking. My career was about to take off. I married my beautiful wife. Both she and I were making very good money with the future looking very bright. However, as Christ said, "It is harder for a camel to go through and eye of a needle than a rich man enter into heaven." Whether you believe as some theologians do that Christ was talking about the very small city gates that required a camel to get down on its knees to get it or a literal eye of a sowing needle the point is the same, we tend to forget about God when things are going well for us.

How Much Longer, Lord?

✦ ✦ ✦ ✦ ✦ ✦

B y the year 2000, I had lost six more promotions to P-III or as some police departments would call it the rank of corporal. My nemesis, Captain K—despite the fact that I had a superior court judge openly declare that she was not trustworthy or in his belief non-factual in her representations of me and allegations against me—was promoted to the rank of Commander of LAPD West Bureau. Now she was my new captain's boss. You see, promotions for sergeant or detective went through the human resource and personnel process but a step up in grade (such as corporal) was considered a pay grade advancement and not a promotion. Normally you have an in-house oral interview by a couple of sergeants and you get scored out of one hundred. The top three names was given to the captain of the division you were assigned to for consideration for each opening and pay grade advancement. The captain's choice then went up to bureau level where affirmative action issues could be addressed if the department was looking to advance certain ethnicities or genders. However, nine times out of ten, the bureau commanders let the divisional captains choose who they wanted to advance since they would be still working under their authority and they could tailor these advancements to the individual needs of each division. Not in my case. I worked hard, studied hard, and kept coming in with top scores on my promotional oral interviews only for them to be overturned at the bureau level once Commander K saw my name as my captain's pick.

The extent and the vastness of the conspiracy against me became evident in March of 2000 when I sought outside help and went to the inspector general's office. This office was set up post Rodney King and more recently the Rampart scandal. It was supposed to be separate and isolated from the LAPD chain of command to prevent influence and promote transparency. An employee should be able to theoretically go to the inspector general's office to report concerns of misconduct or retaliation with total anonymity from the LAPD managerial system. Part of the reason for creating this office was the draconian discipline system put into place by Chief Bernard Parks and his successors in office. This environment that they created became such a hostile environment that officers were afraid to report misconduct especially among leadership and command staff. The day of my appointment, I took my wife with me for moral support. She was also a victim of this because it affected both our lives not just financially but our emotional health and stability of our marriage.

I was astounded at what I saw when I arrived in his office. The Inspector General was supposed to be an important position within the Los Angeles Police Department. A position that brought civilian oversight and accountability and perhaps most of all authenticity and transparency to the LAPD. What I saw was an embarrassment. However, before I describe what I saw, I want the reader to understand just what kind of issues the inspector general was dealing with. Here is an example headline from a local media outlet concerning this issue: "The LA Police Commission met at LAPD headquarters downtown to address Inspector General Alexander Bustamante's employment litigation audit. The June 27 report revealed that the LAPD destroys case files, keeps inaccurate and incomplete information on lawsuits, and has no system to learn from workplace liability claims. In six years the city spent $110 million in jury awards or settlements for lawsuits involving LAPD personnel, the inspector general said. Of that amount, $31 million, or 28 percent, was spent on claims involving sexual harassment, retaliation and discrimination" (Los Angeles Times).

The Office of the Inspector General (OIG) is one of the major Christopher Commission reform recommendations. The recommendation was to place a civilian with no connection to the department in a position to monitor, audit, and oversee the department's disciplinary system. The position of inspector general is exempt from civil service and reports directly to the Board of Police Commissioners. The receipt and review of citizen complaints of misconduct and oversight of the department's internal disciplinary system are also important functions of the board. Chief Parks didn't hide the fact that he despised the office of inspector general. He saw it as an abatement on his authority to run the department. So I should not have been surprised when I went to the inspector general's office and saw that they had him set up in essentially what looked like an old broom closet. The walls to his office were only about seven feet high which didn't run all the way to the ceiling so that there was about a three-foot gap on all four sides of his office partitions. It was a small room within a larger room almost like you might find a small conference room within a much larger room or floor but this was no conference room. There, right outside his door, sat an LAPD sergeant who could see anyone coming or going into the inspector's office. My wife and I walked in and were greeted by Inspector General Jeffrey Eglash. He closed the door and had us sit down. What he did next was very telling. He looked at me and my wife and put his finger to his lips and said "Shhhhhh!" He then said in a voice a little louder than a whisper, "The walls have ears," pointing to the three-foot gap in the walls which made it very easy for anyone outside his office to eavesdrop on the entire conversation. This was a very ominous sign. If the inspector general didn't trust the LAPD, what did that say about it? I went on to discuss all the issues that I had gone through with the LAPD and how I had been the victim of a conspiracy to violate my rights under 42 USC 1983, as well as retaliation for bringing forth misconduct and criminal activity that I am mandated to do under state and federal law as well as policy.

After about an hour of conversation, the inspector kindly told my wife and myself that he would look into the allegations but that sometimes he finds it difficult to get the LAPD to cooperate in his investigations. It took about six months before we heard back from the Inspector and I got a letter stating in relevant part that "while the claims you made are serious and troubling, I cannot find enough evidence to substantiate your claims." After I contacted him in response to what seemed like a form letter, he stated that everywhere he went inside LAPD, he was stonewalled when he tried to get answers. I shouldn't have been so surprised.

Two Miracles

+ + + + + +

E ven though it seemed like God was nowhere in sight concerning my career, He was very busy in my personal life and was about to create two miracles in my life. My wife and I had been married now for going on six years and have been trying to get pregnant ever since. My wife has pretty severe endometriosis which is an often painful disorder in which tissue that normally lines the inside of the uterus—the endometrium—grows outside the uterus (endometrial implant). Endometriosis most commonly involves a woman's ovaries, bowel, or the tissue lining your pelvis. In endometriosis, displaced endometrial tissue continues to act as it normally would—it thickens, breaks down, and bleeds with each menstrual cycle. Because this displaced tissue has no way to exit your body, it becomes trapped. In her case, it also involved the ovaries, which causes cysts called endometriomas to form. The endometriosis caused her pain especially during her period.

We had tried a number of procedures including injections of human chorionic gonadotropin (better known as HCG). This drug is made from the urine of pregnant women and injected back into a woman is supposed to increase the amount of eggs produced at ovulation thereby increasing the chance of pregnancy. It is sometimes blamed for multiple births such as twins. They also injected me with HCG as well. In men, HCG is supposed to increase testosterone production and increase sperm count. We tried this a number of times but it didn't work. We tried a host of other procedures including in vitrolization and other drugs. You might ask at this point "Were you praying about it?" The answer is yes and no. I am a born again, spirit-filled Christian who has a very close relationship with the Lord. My wife is Roman Catholic. Her family is originally from Egypt and immigrated here when she was two years old to flee Muslim persecution. Their family is Egyptian Orthodox. When I first met my wife, on our very first date I told her that I was a born again Christian, that I went to church, worked in the ministry part-time, I tithed and believed that the Bible was the inerrant word of God. She said that she also believed in God and was raised going to church. That was good enough for me. I was still a baby Christian and had not matured enough to understand the deep differences between fundamental Protestants and Roman Catholicism (just ask the Irish). When we were dating, my wife came to church with me, watched me serve in the ministry, go to Bible study, tithe, and even abstain from sex during our courtship. Once we got married however, the differences started to show. I am convinced that Catholics are good people but simply not spirit-filled. They go to catechism and confirmation and at the age of fourteen their ticket to heaven is punched and then they go on with their lives with a lot of guilt and allegiance to the Roman Catholic Church—not Jesus. They are never taught to be born again and give their life to Christ and receive the Holy Spirit. I would ask my wife if she believes in Jesus Christ as her Lord and Savior and she will nod her head yes. Yet at the same time she didn't feel it was necessary to go to church, read the bible, spend time in prayer or any of the things that the Spirit drives most Christians to do to complete His primary purpose—to conform us to the image of Jesus Christ.

So while I spent a lot of time volunteering in church (and eventually earning a master's degree in theology), going to church, reading my Bible, and getting up at 3 a.m. to spend time with the Lord, she saw no purpose in that. So I prayed alone about the spiritual things of our life and our needs. Finally, after trying to have a baby for six years and trying everything that man had to offer, I had an epiphany—give God a try. In the Bible, the Apostle John tells us that "Whatever we ask for according to His will He will give us" (John 14:13). James says that "You have not because you ask not" (James 4:2). The Bible also says that "Whenever two or more are gathered together in my name, there I am there among their midst" (Matthew 18:20). Having these scriptures in mind, one night I convinced my wife to pray along side of me at the foot of our bed. This is one of the first times that I can remember us praying together. We prayed for God to give us a child. A very concise but heartfelt prayer that we joined together in. Within ten days of the prayer, she was pregnant. God was showing me again that He loves me and that He answers the prayers of His saints. God also wants to get the credit when miracles happen. This is why He often waits until the day before we get evicted or the day before a divorce is finalized before He acts. Once man has exhausted all of his efforts and it seems impossible, God goes to work. A few months before my wife got pregnant, the gynecologist put her on an experimental medication to stop her periods in an effort to help her endometriosis. The doctor told us not to worry about my wife getting pregnant because it would be impossible for her to get pregnant while on this particular drug. I think this is why God waited until only he could get credit for the miracle.

What I also find is that whenever you step out in faith, the enemy likes to come in and attack. Let me go back to the Parable of the Sower and the Seeds for a moment. Look at the seed which is the Word of God that gets thrown on the path. Immediately the birds (birds are many times a sign of evil or judgment in the Bible) swoop in and eat it before it takes root. This circumstance just doesn't happen in the life of a new believer but in mature ones as well. We tend to think of this parable as when people first hear the Word of God and accept Jesus Christ as their savior that the enemy soon comes into their life and through subterfuge and his tricks he causing things to happen in our life to make us doubt God. When you are a new believer, all you hear are the good things. "Give your life to Christ and all your troubles will be over." This is a common theme among many denominations and pastors, especially those that are seeker-friendly. There is also the prosperity gospel which is a perversion of the true gospel. However, speaking empirically, I find that just the opposite is true. Before a person is saved, they have no spiritual enemies. They are no threat to the devil. You can't get a used demon to chase them. Once you have accepted Jesus Christ as your Lord and Savior, however, you now have a fierce enemy that goes around like a roaring lion looking to pounce. When you see people like Gregg Laurie, who has spent most of his life preaching the gospel and organizing the Harvest Crusades and has contributed to saving millions of souls, lose his son in a tragic accident some people wonder if God is just. "What kind of God would let me get cancer?" "What kind of God would let me lose my career, my house, my marriage, etc.?" This type of thinking is common in an immature believer who has not grown roots and can have a devastating effect. However, as I said, it also happens to those of us that have been in the faith a long time as well. The paradox is that real faith, mature and Spirit-led, mainly comes from hardships. God, at least in my life, has put me through many trials. Trials that I did not want to go through. However, each trial brought a new level of maturity and dependents on God for everything in my life. As humans, we want to be in control of our lives and take credit for achievements. Contrasts this with God wanting us to be humble and totally dependent upon Him. "Dear friends, do not be surprised at the fiery ordeal that has come on you to test you, as though something strange were happening to you" (1 Peter 4:12). Even more directly Peter says "In all this you greatly rejoice though now for a little while you may have had to suffer grief in all kinds of trials. These have come so that the proven genuineness of your faith—of greater worth than gold, which perishes even though refined by fire—may result in praise, glory and honor when Jesus Christ is revealed" (1 Peter 6-9). Lastly, James speaks about trials by saying "Consider it pure joy, my brothers, whenever you face trials of many kinds, because you know that the testing of your faith develops perseverance. Perseverance must finish its work so that you may be mature and complete, not lacking anything" (James 1: 2-4). Accordingly, we can have confidence that having trials in our lives is normal. How we respond to these trials will determine how much we grow and mature in the Lord. Remember, even in these trials God is with us because He promised to never leave us or forsake us.

Of course my wife and I were overjoyed with the news of her pregnancy. We gave full credit to God and rejoiced, and then the enemy went to work. As soon as we had the amniocentesis, the doctor warned of a side effect caused by a fertilization drug that my wife was on at the time. So now we had to live out the rest of the pregnancy trusting God but also with some apprehensiveness in our impending arrival. However, the point is that we trusted God and He did a miracle for us. The doctors had declared us absolutely infertile and I think that was what God wanted. God wants us to run out of all human options so that only he can get the credit for it. God is never late and doesn't stick to our schedules. This would be an ever more present theme in my life over the next fifteen years as God caused me to grow and depend on Him more and more by causing circumstances in my life to be tough. Rachel Lauren Brooks was born on January 21, 1999 at six pounds, ten ounces, and was twenty-one inches long. A perfect baby girl.

My wife and I knew we wanted more kids so the doctors told us that we should try again right away since my wife had just given birth and everything was "open." Sure enough, ten months later, my wife was pregnant with are next child—my son. This is when God decided to drop another miracle on my lap. It was the fall of 2000 and we would soon be a family of four and growing so we needed to put down roots. My wife was originally from Egypt and had lived in the greater Los Angeles area her whole life. I was from a small town in Massachusetts and had been living in the greater Los Angeles for about twelve years now. We were determined not to raise our kids in Los Angeles and especially let them go to the Los Angeles Unified School District system. We were living in an apartment that my wife's father owned and were living rent-free. However, we wanted to have at least two maybe three more children and a 600-square foot apartment wasn't going to cut it. We had managed to save about $45,000, and we figured our price range for a new home was around $375,000 in total back in 2000. We spent three months looking (mostly my wife) for a house to buy all the way north to West Lake Village to all the way south to Mission Viejo. Keep in mind I would have to commute to Los Angeles for at least the next ten to fifteen years. However, I was determined to wait upon the Lord, knowing He would go ahead of us and provide for us. One day after looking at about thirty houses so far, my wife was in Costa Mesa. She, like me, did not know much about Costa Mesa except that it was sandwiched between Newport Beach and Huntington Beach. She was driving around and stopped to talk to an old man named Don who was a real estate agent in his late 70s.

As it turned out, my wife had just gotten a job at the Veterans Administration as a medical claims examiner and Don was an old War World II veteran pilot who had also fought in Korea and Vietnam. He showed my wife a house in a nice area of Costa Mesa called Mesa Verde that was pretty big for this area (approximately 2,600-square feet) that had five bedrooms, three bathrooms and a three-car garage. It was big but needed some work. When my wife inquired about the sale price, Don told my wife that it was on the market for $500,000. This was $125,000 over our affordable price range. My wife called me and described it to me and then told me the price. I told her that I had feeling about this house and to just put in a ridiculous offer of $375,000.00. Don laughed at our suggestion but went along with it and submitted a bid for the house for $375,000.00. This was at the beginning of October of 2000. About a month later, my wife and I were in Las Vegas and I remember distinctly because it was Veterans Day. My wife answered her cell phone and it was Don the broker. She sounded both excited and confused at the same time. I heard her say "Really, are you sure?" My wife put down the phone for a minute and looked at me and said, "You know that big yellow house I was telling you about (I had never seen it)? I said "The one you told me about on the cul de sac and with five bedrooms within walking distance to the ocean?" She said "Yeah, that one." "What about it?" I inquired. "You remember how it was on the market for $500,000 and you told me just to throw in a ridiculous offer of $375,000?" I said "Yeah." She said, "They accepted it!" She got back on the phone with the broker Don and said "We'll take it." Don didn't want to sell the house to us because he knew I had never seen it. I got on the phone with Don and said "Don, go ahead and open escrow, I don't need to see it, it's from the Lord." Turns out that this house was a divorce sale and the parents were going through a nasty divorce and their four teenage kids were living there almost unsupervised. The house was being sold as part of the divorce settlement but the husband kept sabotaging the sale. The judge ordered him to take the next offer they got which was ours! How good is God? We waited upon His timing and he went ahead of us and made the crooked paths straight. It reminds me of the Prophet Isaiah who said that "Since ancient times no one has heard, no ear has perceived, no eye has seen any God besides you, *who acts on behalf of those who wait for him*" (Isaiah 64: 4) Emphases added. We moved in New Year's Day 2001.

Besides the house and two children God gave us, 2001 did not start out well for me with LAPD. The retaliation now continued into its seventh year. The denial of work permits, some more denial of promotions. I was going to work every day and they were looking for any excuse to terminate me. By this time, I had been under constant acts of retaliation, loss of promotions, denial of overtime, denial of work permits, denial of assignments, and my health had started to take a turn for the worse from all the stress which would later lead to my death. I have always tried to look at things from the bigger picture and from God's point of view. Sometimes we don't understand what He is doing in our life. Sometimes we question whether or not He is listening to us or cares. Scripture makes it abundantly clear that the answer to the above to questions is in the affirmative. Still, when in the middle of a storm, we tend to take our eyes off of Him and onto our circumstances which is a big mistake and the goal of our enemy. God had already begun to deal with some of the issues in my life and started to put in me a desire to develop a much closer relationship with Him and to give me guidance for the future. Little did I know what God was about to do in my life.

I have often heard in my Christian walk from pastors that it is important to develop the ability to listen to God. I use to think that it was just for pastors of elders or maybe people with the gift of tongues and those in the ministry. The ability to listen to God. We see in the Old Testament God speak to men of God like Noah, Moses, Jacob Abraham, and many others. We also see in the New Testament God or Jesus, God incarnate, speaking to Peter, Paul and Mary (not the band) among others. I never really thought about learning to listen to God's still small voice. I had been led by the Spirit many times but not heard directly from God. I do remember vividly when

God brought me to San Diego, California and how the Holy Spirit directed me to Los Angeles and right to the Wilshire Division as I discussed earlier. However, that didn't prepare me for what was about to happen next. So God, who had just blessed my wife and me with two children after being declared infertile, had also just given us the house of our dreams for dirt cheap. We bought the new house in December of 2000 but there was four teenage children living there apparently almost unsupervised and they wanted one last Christmas in their home. So I granted their wish and we didn't take possession until January of 2001. The house needed a lot of work so we took a $50,000 second mortgage and started hiring contractors to do the work. The house was not ready for all of us to live in with a lot of dust and some mold because of all the construction going on. So my wife and our two-year-old and one year old children lived with my wife's parents who had purchased a house about three blocks away one year earlier. I, however, wanted to keep an eye on things so I slept upstairs in the new house while it was being renovated. At the time, I was still working Pacific Division of LAPD so I was now commuting forty-three miles one way to work every day. I had also just purchased a new Chevy Tahoe (well, sort of new; it had 10,000 miles on it) that got about sixteen miles to the gallon. At that time, the LAPD had not gone to the 3/12 compressed work schedule and those of us in patrol were still working traditional eight-hour days. I was assigned to what was call "PM Watch." This is from 3 p.m. until around 11 p.m. It was my favorite shift because you got home at a reasonable time of about midnight and could sleep in and have the mornings and early afternoons off to conduct personal business or work out.

The Lord Finally Speaks

✦ ✦ ✦ ✦ ✦ ✦

One early afternoon before I was about to take off for my daily commute of forty-three miles one way from Costa Mesa to Los Angeles to work, I decided to pray and spend some time in my office speaking to God. As I said, despite all of the miracles God had done in my personal life, I had now been going through about six or seven years of absolute turmoil within LAPD. Six years earlier my career was about to take off and then it was cut short all because I did the right thing. It is very important that I describe to you the circumstances around me at the time so what I am about to tell you can only be credited to God's glory. First off, I was alone. I was living in the house alone as previously mentioned and there were no contractors or workers present in the house or even outside around the house. The windows to the office in my house were shut and locked as was all the doors and windows because I had already locked everything preparing to go to work. I went into my office and closed the door. I got down on my knees. I started out with a simple prayer of forgiveness for my sins but my soul was tormented. I was worn down from the constant harassment from LAPD. I cried out to the Lord and I said to Him, "Lord, I know you brought me three thousand miles from my home to work as a police officer for LAPD. I know it was you that saved my life and supernaturally healed me twice when I should have been dead. I know it was you and you only that allowed me to have children and blessed us with a house we had no right to have or could afford. But Lord, why are You putting me through this test? Surely you didn't make me leave my career back in Massachusetts and everything and all my family to come out here alone so that I could go through this misery. Surely this cannot be part of your plan. You are God and can do anything so I need to know Lord. I need to know what your plan and purpose (Jeremiah 29:11) is for my life. Lord I want to know and I want to know by the end of the day. I want to know today what Your plan and purpose is for me." I was weeping and crying pretty well throughout this prayer but I had done something I had never done before—make a demand of God. I was very specific in saying that I wanted to know His plan for my life and I wanted to know by the end of the day or before tomorrow. It is probably foolish to demand something of God. I do believe that we can come to Him with His promises he gives us in the Bible and remind Him of them. Like His promise to provide for us. I am not so sure the wisdom about making demands to the very God who holds my next breath in His hands or who had just blessed me with a house and children. Still, I think we all want to know, at least at some points in our lives, what God's plan and purpose is for us. Most of us want to be in the middle of His will but how can we if we don't know what it is?

I came home that evening from a pretty uneventful shift with LAPD. Nothing memorable happened. I got home about 11:30 p.m. or perhaps a little bit later but I was tired and I went right to bed. Once again, I was living alone in the house. I actually slept in my bedroom that night and not on the couch as had been my habit. It was about one o'clock in the morning and I was in a deep sleep and I heard the Lord say to me "Get up." I was dazed and scared. This was not an audible voice but it was even clearer than if God was speaking to me audibly. "What is it Lord?" I responded knowing immediately who was speaking to me. "Go downstairs," I remember God's voice telling me. So I found myself downstairs in my house at one o'clock in the morning, alone and in my t-shirt and shorts and little dazed. The Lord then said to me "Go outside." I hesitated for a moment but then opened my front door and walked to the front iron gate. I could see my new Chevy Tahoe in the drive way. I had just purchased the car a few months before. Then the Lord said to me, "Look." I looked through the small holes of the mesh screen covering the iron gate and saw through the passenger compartment front window something sticking to the driver's side window. I couldn't identify it. I opened the gate and walked across the driveway in the dark. As I grew closer to the driver's window, I saw that the object looked like a folded piece of paper. Sure enough, it was a piece of paper sticking in between the window and the window frame. I grabbed it and carefully unfolded it. I took a quick look around to see if someone was maybe playing a joke on me or whoever had placed the paper on my car was still nearby but I saw no one. It was a hand written note that said: "This is God's answer to your prayer today: John 3:19." I stared at it and read it a couple of times until it suddenly hit me. What did I ask God for? His purpose and plan for my life. All of a sudden the magnitude of realizing that the God of the universe, the God that created the Heavens and the Earth, the God that sent His only son to earth to die for me, had condescended Himself to give me a note telling me above all things that He was listening to me. That He cared enough about a puny creature like me to reach out to me and tell me that yes, yes indeed He had a plan for me. Of course then the enemy started coming at me saying to my conscious that someone probably just overheard me praying and wrote the note. Not possible. There was no one around in the house or outside the house and the windows and doors were closed and locked. I do believe that the Lord used a prophet or someone that had the gift of the Word of Knowledge and led them to put this note on my car after directing what was to be written on it. After all, what is scripture but Holy Spirit inspired writings written by men selected by God. Moses wrote the Pentateuch and Paul wrote most of the New Testament as directed by the Holy Spirit.

Once I kind of got over the shock of getting a memo from God, my mind then started to think of what the message meant. Every Christian knows John 3:16, but what about John 3:19? I confess I didn't have it memorized. I ran back into my house and grabbed my Bible—both my NIV and my King James versions. John 3:19 says "This is the verdict: Light has come into the world, but men loved darkness instead of light because their deeds were evil." What did this mean? The general application I think is pretty obvious. Jesus is saying that God sent Him into the world to be the light or salvation for mankind but He was rejected because people would rather enjoy darkness which is a euphemism for sin or evil. That much is pretty clear. However, what does it mean in application to me? I was going to church, volunteering in the ministry, reading my Bible and doing everything I thought a Christian should be doing. I began to look at it using duality. Duality is very common in the Bible. For example, many prophecies are dual in nature. Throughout the Bible, we see duality in many things. God made a material creation and a spiritual creation (Genesis 2:1-4). The first Adam was physical, and the second Adam, Christ, is spiritual (I Corinthians 15:45-47). The Old Covenant was based on physical descent and physical blessings and cursing. It was followed by the New Covenant, which is spiritual (Hebrews 8). At the first coming of Christ, He came in the weakness of flesh; when He comes again, He will be a powerful spirit being.

So the first interpretation I had was that I was living with one foot in God's kingdom and one foot in man' kingdom. Perhaps I wasn't totally committed to God as I should be. I don't mean that I was lukewarm but that there may have been areas in my life that were not totally surrendered to God. God demands that every area of our life be surrendered over to Him. Not to be judgmental but I do find it comical if not paradoxical that many Christians trust God with their eternal soul but not with their money. I know the arguments over tithing. Those who support it quote Malachi 3:8. They say that it is the only time in scripture that God asks us to test Him. Those opposed say that it was an Old Testament system for tithing that actually predates the Mosaic system of law (Genesis 14:18-20). My personal belief is more in line of what Paul says in Corinthians when he says, "The point is this: whoever sows sparingly will also reap sparingly, and whoever sows bountifully will also reap bountifully. Each one must give as he has decided in his heart, not reluctantly or under compulsion, for God loves a cheerful giver" (2 Corinthians 9:6-7). The law of reciprocity is the important fact—reaping what we sew. Nevertheless, I had to re-examine my heart and commitment to Christ. When I thought about it, there was a bit of idolatry going on in my life that I hadn't quite realized. Back in 1995, I was about to become one of the youngest sergeants in LAPD history tenure wise. Back then it was very rare to see officers make sergeant with less than ten years of seniority. I told myself the usual stuff about how making sergeant will allow me to help other officers stay out of trouble and how I would be a better role model for God etc. However, it was about ego. It had now been six years since I should have made sergeant twice and detective once, not to mention P-III (corporal) several times. I was putting making sergeant ahead of God. I even went so far as to drop out of my PhD program I had just started and went to law school to learn how to fight the LAPD and the City of Los Angeles. I was putting my career ahead of God but rationalizing it by thinking that it must be God's will for me to promote since He is the one that brought me three thousand miles and established me in the LAPD. It wasn't the only issue as my reputation re-established was also important to me but the promotion was idolatrous. So I felt that this could be one application of God's John 3:19 answer to my prayer. I also didn't think that it was the entire application since I had asked God what His plan and purpose for my life were. Again, using duality, I saw this scripture as futuristic as well. A call to evangelism could also be an accurate interpretation of this scripture.

Thus my second application was to the issue of evangelism. Was this a foretelling from God that He was going to use me to rescue those in darkness into the light? I was pretty open about my faith even in the LAPD which has a spirit of anti-Christ. I believe it is the main reason they were trying to get rid of me and retaliating against me day after day. By this point in my battle with LAPD, I could sense the spirit of evil indwelt in it. I can vividly remember on several occasions when I was making the forty-three-mile commute to work. I was usually listening to KWAVE or KKLA, both Christian radio stations and as soon as I drove my car into the parking lot of the police station I could feel this heaviness come over me. It is hard to describe. Sort of like a spirit of depression. The Bible talks about demonic principalities and kingdoms like when Michael fought against the Prince of Persia to get a massage to the prophet Daniel (Daniel 10:13). It would not surprise me if the Los Angeles Police Department had a demonic spirit assigned to it. Homosexuality was prevalent. Self-centered egocentric individualism as well. Lots of guys cheating on their wives. I had met quite a few professing Christians in LAPD but they were more like closet Christians. In fact, most of the damage done to me within LAPD was done to me by so called Christians. Many of them sell out their faith in order to advance their careers.

Still, I could have been more evangelic towards others. I think the hardest part for me in evangelizing within the LAPD is that I had let some of the stress and workplace issues get to me. I was forced for several years to work the most stressful place possible—the front desk. Other officers come to the station and even from outside divisions to book prisoners or property and they see you working the front desk and think you are either lazy or incompetent or both. It is true that some officers just don't want to work "the field" and want to just collect a paycheck and go home without the dangers associated with patrol or the overtime and court. The general reputation of a desk officer was demeaning. I had let some of these things get to me and I was always breathing law suits and hatred toward the LAPD administration and management. Hard to tell people they need Christ when you are complaining all the time about work, your boss, and seem just plain miserable.

However, the fact remained that the living God of the Universe had spoken to me. Even if the message was not exactly clear to me or will be revealed later down the road (which it has) the fact remains that He spoke to me. I had to be careful because after I started to get over the initial shock of it all, I started to become a little conceded. I thought about framing the note. I thought about showing it off. Then I remembered what the Apostle Paul had said. Paul was privileged by God to see things most people will never see until they get to heaven. The Lord knew that these types of privileges can make us puffed up in the flesh and conceited. Paul was given a thorn in his side—a messenger from Satan. We don't really know what it was. Some people speculate that it was his eyesight since he was blinded by the Lord for three days until something like scales fell off his eyes. However, we really don't know. I decided to rip the note up. I didn't want to become prideful and full of conceitedness. I already had the scripture memorized and I know who the note was from. That's all that mattered. I did pray for confirmation about the message and I got it.

About six months later, after receiving the note from the Lord, I had signed up for a long-term disability and death insurance policy. A month before, I was supposed to have a nurse come to my house to draw blood and urine before the policy would be approved I ended up cancelling the policy because we couldn't afford it. Accordingly, I was surprised when I was home alone one day and I heard my door bell ring. I answered the door and saw a young lady there on my front steps wearing a medical I.D. around her neck holding what I recognized as a blood drawing kit. See told me that she was there to collect blood and urine for my life insurance policy. I apologized and explained to her that we had cancelled the policy about a month before because we couldn't afford it. She looked right at me intensely and stated, "That's ok, the Lord has given me a word of knowledge for you." She went on to tell me that the Lord had a specific plan and purpose for me and that He wanted me to do two things: step out in faith and get my house in order. This would be a recurring theme for me repeated several times over the next decade. I have to admit, it was one thing to get a note left on my car by the Lord in the middle of the night but quite another for another human being to come to my house claimed to be sent of God. Here is the best part about the whole thing. My whole spiritual life which started at the age of twenty-three, God has gone out of His way to give me both clear direction and confirmation that it was Him who was speaking to me. So as I was listening to this woman on my door step telling me a message she had from God for me in the back of my head I was wondering to myself, *Is this lady a nut job or is she really a God send?* I mean, who wouldn't? At least the first time anyway. Later in my walk with the Lord this type of thing would become more common place as I also developed a stronger ability to listen to the Lord's voice.

So just as I was thinking this, she started to walk away and then suddenly turned around and looked right at me and said, "Just so you know that what I am saying is from the Lord, when I leave, go inside you house and turn on your stereo." Seriously. This is exactly what she said. How did she know that I even had a stereo? We had just moved the family into the house we had bought not too long ago. I had just taken the stereo out of boxes and set it up next to the dining room table. I hadn't even bothered to program the channels or preset them. However, I did what I was told. I closed the door still staring at this woman rather quizzically. I walked over to the stereo and just simply flicked the switch. The stereo came blaring to life. I listened intently having an idea in the back of my mind that I was only going to give it about ten seconds of listening before I would turn it off. All of a sudden, I heard a pastor's voice on the radio and could tell it was some type of sermon or discourse. I heard the following words come from the stereo speakers: "The Lord wants two things of you: and step out in faith and get your house in order." Is it possible for a person's jaw to drop all the way to the ground? I listened more intently but a commercial came on and I just walked over to the front window to look out to see if the woman was still there. She wasn't.

This whole incident reminded me of 2 Kings 20: 7-11 in which God had just told Hezekiah through the prophet Isaiah that he was going to die. Hezekiah weeps and reminds the Lord that he has served Him faithfully his whole life. God changes His mind and tells Hezekiah (through Isaiah) that he will heal him, give him fifteen more years of life and deliver him from the Assyrians. Hezekiah asks God for a sign of confirmation that He would do as He says. Isaiah says to Hezekiah: "This is the Lord's sign to you that the Lord will do what He has promised: Shall the shadow go forward ten steps or back ten steps." Knowing that the sun would naturally go forward during the course of the days, Hezekiah picked the one in which could only be accredited to God's supernatural ability which would be for the sun to go in reverse or the shadow moving backwards. Likewise, God gave me confirmation that this was Him who was speaking to me. I didn't ask Him for confirmation (yet) but I was thinking about it when the woman beat me to the punch and told me to turn on my stereo. Going forward this would be a consistent theme in my life. God has always been good about giving me confirmation when I come to making major decisions in my life or responding to a word of knowledge He has given me.

The First Prophet

I f in reading the above narrative about God leaving me a note on my car window in response to my prayer request to Him to reveal His plan and purpose for me or at least to reconfirm it left you a little skeptical, this next encounter may be even more difficult for you to believe or understand. Having just recently been given a tremendous boost to my spirit by being given a word of knowledge from the Lord, I wasn't expecting another word of knowledge, this time from a prophetess. A few months go by after receiving the note from the Lord and while incredibly grateful and a boost to my spirit I guess I needed more convincing.

My wife and I had decided to get me some life insurance now that we had two children and some assets. We contacted an insurance company and made arrangements to procure a policy. If you have ever had a life insurance policy, then you know that standard procedure is that they send a nurse or hematologist lab technician to your home to collect blood and urine. I think this is to see if you are a smoker or not and probably to check other health related issues. They normally take your height and weight, blood pressure, urine sample, and blood sample. At times, an EKG will also be required for older clients or for clients looking to get a large amount of life insurance coverage. The examiner will also inquire into who your primary care physician is as well as any other doctors you have seen recently. Finally, the examiner will request your see driver's license for identification purposes. So this is the process I was waiting to go through after applying for a life insurance policy. However, before the visit to my house took place we decided to cancel it because it was too expensive and a cash policy which was risky. That was the end of the matter as far as I was concerned. But not God. A few weeks after giving notice of the cancellation of the intent to obtain a life insurance policy, my doorbell rang. Again, I was home and alone. I answered the door and I saw a middle aged woman in a white lab coat holding a bin with what looked like small glass vials. I immediately recognized her as someone from the insurance company. I told her that I was sorry but we had cancelled the policy a few weeks before. She looked me straight in the eye and said "That's ok, that's not why I am really here. I have a word of knowledge for you from the Lord." I just kind of looked at her for a minute, trying to digest and comprehend what she had just told me. Seeing how God had just done a bevy of miracles in my life over the last few years and that He had just caused a note to be left on my car in answer to a prayer, this didn't seem too far outside of the realm of possibilities. "What do you have to tell me?" I said. She said the following, "The Lord wants you to get your house in order and step out in faith." Now there were some other things she said but that was the gist of it. To be honest, in my mind I was still wondering if this lady, this prophetess was for real was she was speaking to me. She then turned and started to walk down the pathway to the front gate and the driveway when she suddenly stopped. She paused quietly momentarily as if being spoken to by an angel or the Holy Spirit. She then turned around and looked intently at me and said, "Just so you know that what I am telling you is from the Lord, after I leave turn on your stereo." I stood there for a few moments, gathering my wits. Who has a prophet sent to them by God? I mean this is not the Old Testament in which God appeared to Moses or had his prophets' prophesize to Israel's kings or about judgment. This was little old me. A nobody. I am not Billy Graham or Charles Stanley or Chuck Smith. Maybe this was the point. The Apostle Paul said to the Corinthian Church, "Brothers and sisters, think of what you were when you were called. Not many of you were wise by human standards; not many were influential; not many were of noble birth. But God chose the foolish things of the world to shame the wise; God chose the weak things of this world of the world to shame the strong; God chose lowly things of this world and the despised things—and the things that are not—to nullify the things that are, so that no one may boast before Him" (I Corinthians 1:26-30). Unwise, weak, not noble, uninfluential, lowly—this I can identify with.

In the Old Testament the test of a true prophet was whether or not their prophecy came true. If it didn't, they would be stoned to death. In my case, the confirmation would come from her edict to turn on my stereo. I thought it a strange request but no stranger than a prophetess showing up at my door. I had just moved in the house two months earlier and had unpacked the stereo just the day before. I had not tuned it or set the stations. I hadn't even plugged it in. So I walked over to the living room, plugged in the stereo and flipped the switch. The stereo came to life and on came a pastor who was in the middle of a sermon and said almost word for word what she had told me "Get your house in order and step out in faith." I planned on doing just that.

The False Prophet

❖❖❖❖❖

I would be negligent in my duty to warn anyone reading this book not to discuss one of the most regretful chapters in my spiritual life—the false prophet. Remember this is 2003 and although I was still being harassed for eight years now by the LAPD, God had showed up in a big way. I was just coming off of the last three years in which God had left me a note on my car in response to a prayer for His plan for my life, reaffirmed it by sending me a word of knowledge through a prophetess, allowed us to have children when we were declared infertile, gave us a wonderful house we should not have been able to afford, and there were many other smaller blessings. I guess I just started to expect the unexpected miracles and interventions of God as a common thing.

One day I was at a gym that a friend of mine, Ray, had built and opened in Marina del Rey. I had known him when I was training and competing at Gold's Gym in Venice, California nearby. He knew that I was a Christian and one day introduced me to a man I will call Randy. Randy was a former bodybuilder who was now making money as "Duke Nukem" the famous 1990s video game. He looked just like him. He was big, a little bigger than me but not quite as muscular at about six feet three inches and two hundred sixty pounds, crop-top short blonde hair, and even wore the patented sunglasses. As soon as Ray introduced me to him at the gym, he looked right at me and told me that he had had a vision the night before from God and that He was supposed to mentor me. Again, on its face and taken individually it sounded absurd. However, look at what God had legitimately just done in my life. This seemed very consistent with how God had recently operated in my life. In fact, it almost makes sense as the next step in the development of my Christian faith after what God had done and revealed to me for me to be personally mentored. I had never seen anyone walk the walk or talk the Christian talk as much as Randy did. Every time I saw or spoke to him he was fasting or talking about visions and God's plan for Him. He told me that God had put Him in charge of the West Coast and just like demons have regions and kingdoms they rule, he was going to be God's sovereign ruler during the pending last days before Christ return to earth known as the rapture. I look back on it now and can see right through him and what a false teacher and prophet he was. However, I was vulnerable at the time and the enemy knew it. I went to Bible studies in his apartment and started to give him a little bit of money here and there. My wife met him and right away couldn't stand him. I, on the other hand, started to idolize him. He seemed so spiritually-minded and powerful. He talked about how he had rebuked the devil and cast out demons and the laying of strongholds. I had never seen anyone so bold in their faith. Pretty soon however, he wanted money. After all he said, you should tithe to whoever is feeding you spiritually. I was between churches at the time since I had moved from Los Angeles to Orange County so it made sense. My wife warned me again not to hang out with this guy and never give him any money. I soon found myself lying to my wife and making up excuses to hang out with him. Every time we did a one-on-one bible study, he just seemed to open my eyes to the scripture and he truly seemed spirit-filled. After a while I started noticing that I wasn't the only one that he had befriended. In fact, I eventually learned that he had someone paying for his apartment, his car, spending money, his gym membership and had a friend for just about all occasions. He was living pretty high on the hog for someone that didn't work. Still, despite the warning signs, I did something stupid. My wife's parents own two apartment buildings in West Los Angeles. Randy had said that his lease had run out (I later found out he hadn't paid rent in three months). I felt that this was a good opportunity to show the Lord that I was doing His work by taking care of a fellow brother in Christ who also said he was an apostle. I talked my wife who was managing the buildings to let Randy move in.

It didn't take long for things to go sideways. From the time that I had come to know Andy, he kept mentioning his spiritual mentor who lived in Minnesota—a guy named Garry Herzog. Once Randy got established out in Marina del Rey and got some followers, Garry came out with his daughter and started weaving a web of deceit and cult hood. What I mean is, his daughter all of a sudden fell in love with Ray's partner who owned half of the gym. She said it was God's will that they should be married. They got married two weeks from meeting and immediately became pregnant. She then went to work pushing Ray out the door. Soon other relatives and "friends" of Garry's arrived and started getting jobs at the gym and around the local businesses. Randy got married on weekend to a girl he met in Hawaii. I never met her. The way Randy tells it is that he found out she was "impure" after he married her and had to "get rid of her." What I really think happened is that she found out the truth. I think she realized that he was not the man he said he was and saw what he really was—a false teacher and prophet.

Eventually a cult started to take shape and they had their claws into several blocks of business and had everyone believing that this was God's will. Randy came to me one day and told me that he couldn't pay the rent. He was still living in my wife's parent's apartment buildings. He was already two months behind at $1,000.00 a month. He told me that I should be tithing to him. I told him that my wife forbade me from giving him money and I was already getting repercussions for convincing her to put him in the apartment building. I made a second and bigger mistake. I wanted to give Andy the money to pay the rent but how could I do it without my wife finding out? She ran all the finances of the house and the bank accounts. Sometimes I think God puts people in your life for reasons and for seasons. Right at that time, I had a new captain transferred into LAPD Pacific Division. I heard he was a strong Christian man who had recently lost his son. I went in to see him one day in his office. I first established that he was a believer and then, having established that, if he was willing to give me some spiritual and marital advice. I told him that I was torn between doing what I thought God would want me to do (pay Randy's rent) and being deceptive to my wife and essentially lying behind her back. After questioning me and establishing that God had not, in fact, confirmed to me that doing this for Randy was His will he sided with my wife. He said, "God gave you a wife for a reason. Listen to her." Despite this sage advice from my captain that was probably spot on and full of wisdom, I turned from it. I went down to the Los Angeles Police Federal Credit Union and took out a personal signature loan for $2,000. To complete the deception, I made the loan manager promise not to send any loan documents or statements to the house so that my wife would not find out. Payments would come out in small enough portions out of my bimonthly paycheck that she wouldn't notice.

Isn't it funny how God has a way of interrupting even the best plans we make? Even though this was obviously in hindsight a big mistake, it needed to be exposed. The very day I took the money out from the credit union, I got a phone call from my wife who was very irate. At first I played it off as if I didn't know what she was talking about. Then she told me she had received a phone call from the bank manager who wanted to know some information because some of the loan documents were incomplete. I was nailed, caught cold lying to my wife and doing the very thing she had asked me not to do. The very thing I had promised not to do to the woman I had made a covenant to spend the rest of my life with. Still I didn't learn. I was so convinced that God had put Randy in my life to mentor me that I ignored all the warning signs and advice I had received. So I kept sneaking around behind my wife's back in order to spend time with the "apostle." One day, she finally had it. She made me confront him. We drove up to his apartment which was the building owned by my wife's parents and the one in which I had just tried to pay the rent for him with the $2,000. My wife was very upset and sensed that I was choosing him over her. She saw Randy as a threat to our marriage and was going to fight for her marriage. That's what I love about her. I don't think I ever would have chosen to follow this man who calls himself an apostle and prophet of God over my wife unless I directly heard it from God himself. So far this wasn't the case.

My wife went with me into the apartment and was met by Andy who knew we were coming. She pulled up a chair about three feet across from Andy and I sat to the side perpendicular and sort of between both of them. She jumped right in and started screaming at him calling him a thief and not a man of God. I don't remember everything she said to him but I will never forget his response to her. After she gave him a good earful, I was anticipating a cogent response, logical and persuasive. Instead he looked into her eyes and said, "You have a demon in you." He looked at me and said, "Don't you see it Barry? Her eyes are turning red." Well no, I didn't see her eyes turning red except maybe some of the blood vessels popping out from anger. He kept saying louder and louder and pointing to her and saying "Can't you see it?" "That's not her talking, it's the demon." "Look at her eyes!" I thought I had seen and heard everything. I mean, yes, my wife has the Middle Eastern temper and occasional craziness but demon possessed? Anyway, we left that day with a move out date and agreement to wave the back rent if he moved out immediately. The last straw came after I promised my wife (again) that I would never see him again. I had just split a six-million-dollar verdict with about fifteen other police officers for settling a retaliation lawsuit by the LAPD. After attorney's fees, taxes and everything, my cut came to $300,000. More on that later.

Even though I promised my wife I would never see Randy again at the cost of our marriage, I decided to go by and tell him the good news that not only had I been vindicated and had several false complaints thrown out but also got almost a quarter of a million dollars. I knocked on his door which was an apartment in Marina de Rey he got someone else to pay for. He let me in and I told him the good news. He said, "How much, two hundred thousand dollars?" "Hold on." He picked up the phone and dialed a long distance number and then kind of turned his back to me. I heard a lot of "Ah huh. Okay, I'll tell him." Randy hung up the phone and said the following to me: "That was Garry. He said that if you want to continue being a part of this ministry and doing was is right in God's eyes, then give me twenty thousand dollars right now." I looked at him incredulously like I couldn't believe my ears. I had risked my reputation, my marriage and even my career for this guy and all he wanted from me was money. All of a sudden, it finally hit me. What a fool I had been. I looked at him and said, goodbye and walked out the door. I think he was in shock more than I was. I think that he and Garry had been so used to getting anyone to do their bidding. Later on I would hear of people taking second mortgages on their homes to give these people money all because they told them God said to. My friend Ray ended up losing his gym and house. Several other people ended up losing their jobs because as soon as it became known this was a cult, the dominos started to fall. All except Mike. He was dumb enough to marry Larry's daughter within less than a month of meeting him and of course got herself pregnant right away.

The take away lesson that I learned from this incident in my life is that I had to know God's word inside and out. That way I could never be fooled. It is like how they train the secret service agents to spot counterfeit money. They don't show them fake bills or counterfeits, instead they make them so familiar with real American currency and bills that they can spot a fake a mile away. Even now, a little over a decade later, I still get emails once in a while from LinkedIn. Randy has reinvented himself and has a new ministry online that I won't give the name to. However, if you read it, you would think you were reading the sayings of a mad man. The more I stepped back from the situation and as time went by, I started to think that Randy wasn't so much a co-conspirator as partially mentally disturbed individual who was used by an evil person imitating a holy man. I discovered that just before meeting Garry, Randy had had a mental breakdown of some kind. I know he did a lot of drugs bodybuilding and many of those guys from my experience are not well-balanced to begin with. I think Larry was silently in the background as the puppeteer pulling the strings and reaping the benefits. The bottom line is that we need to be so discerning by the Spirit and familiar with God's Word, that we can spot a fake right away. There are many false teachers out there right now looking to dupe naïve Christians—the weak, the sick and the old. From miracle oil, to handkerchiefs you put over your wallet to make money appear; they are charlatans. To people like this, I believe Jesus had this verse in mind when He said, "Many will say to me on that day, 'Lord, Lord, did we not prophesy in your name and in your name drive out demons and in your name perform many miracles?' Then I will tell them plainly, 'I never knew you. Away from me, you evildoers!" (Matthew 7:22-24).

The Class Action

B y the beginning of 2003, things were starting to look up. I had just won the retaliation lawsuit that had dragged on for half a dozen years and part of the agreement in exchange for LAPD admitting no liability (which they never do) they agreed that Captain K (now Commander K) was dishonest and several of the complaints she had filed were not only groundless but patently false. When a federal judge says you have "no credibility" to a commanding officer of LAPD, you would think they would get rid of her. No. Instead, consistent with the paradigm rule of merit, the incompetent get promoted up. The important part was that the agreement stated that the LAPD would "seal" several false complaints in my personnel package. These were complaints that had sullied my reputation. As a Christian, my reputation was very important to me. One of the complaints was that I gave false and misleading information during an interview which was total garbage. However, the command staff were cognizant of the fact that as long as I had a complaint alleging dealing with any type of character issues, such as false and misleading complaint, that this would keep me from promoting. They were desperate to keep me from promoting into supervision and management. To be one of them. What I didn't realize was the subterfuge they were about to employ.

This lawsuit that had just settled involved about fifteen police officers. It was started by Goldberg and Gage law firm with maybe fifty plaintiffs who were mostly police officers, sergeants, and detectives. However, when filing a lawsuit and seeking class action status, there are several things that must be proven in order for the court to grant class action status. This is important for attorneys because under many different statutes, attorneys get paid for bringing class action lawsuits because the courts want to encourage lawyers to take up cases that have hurt perhaps an entire class of people who may not have the money, expertise, or time to bring individual suits. So due to judicial economy and the maxim that every plaintiff should have his day in court, attorneys often can get compensated for bringing class action suits even if they lose the case. For example, Rule 23(a) of the Federal Rules of Civil Procedure, which I studied ad nausea in law school, requires the following facts in order to be granted class action status: numerosity—the class is so numerous that joinder of all members is impracticable; commonality—requires that there are questions of law or fact common to the class. The commonality requirement is generally satisfied in actions in which there is "a single issue common to all members of the class;" typicality—requires that a claim or defenses of the representative parties are typical of the claims or defenses of the class. For example, a claim is "typical" if it arises from the same event or practice or course of conduct that gives rise to the claims of the other class members, and if his or her claims are based on the same legal theory; adequate representation—requires that "the representative parties will fairly and adequately protect the interests of the class." There are two criteria for determining whether the representation of the class will be adequate: 1) the representative must have common interests with unnamed members of the class, and 2) it must appear that the representatives will vigorously prosecute the interest of the class through qualified counsel. Besides being granted class action status, attorneys like to go to federal court because the statutes along with juries allow for bigger verdicts usually. Anytime you are looking at a class action lawsuit and you can prove punitive damages or a violation of constitutionally protected right such as under 42 USC 1983, there are millions to be had.

I had to qualify what I am about to present next with the above information so it will make more sense in its context. Going back to the law suit settlement, as discussed above, it started as a want to be class action lawsuit by Goldberg and Gage. They even had this media event to try to shame the LAPD and Los Angeles City Attorney's Office. They invited all the plaintiffs including me down to their office. I was a little late getting there. As soon as I walked into their office and saw the circus and all the potential plaintiffs, I knew they were in trouble. I looked around and saw black, white, Hispanics, male, female, gay, straight and just about every race, ethnicity, and gender to be had. It was the rainbow coalition. When I started asking some of the plaintiffs what their cases were about, it confirmed my suspicions. Some were suing like me, for retaliation, some for sexual discrimination, hostile work environment, and many other causes. This did not have the characteristics of a class action status lawsuit. Now as it happens, there was a prestigious law firm named Wasserman, Comden & Casselman, L.L.P. From what I understood in a little background on them at the time and from write-ups, they had recently won a multi-billion dollar verdict against big tobacco company in a personal injury case. The rumor was that they saw big money in federal civil rights cases involving police and fire litigation especially under 42 USC1983 statues and they wanted to break into this type of litigation. They came into this case with Goldberg and Gage as co-counsel. Goldberg and Gage had hyped this case and probably presented it to them as a winner. However, to demonstrate how widespread the environment of retaliation was against any officer that challenged the absolute hegemony of LAPD management, Goldberg and Gage also represented three hundred former police officers as well that had been allegedly falsely terminated. Once I arrived at the media session however, like me, I think that the firm of Wasserman, Comden & Casselman realized when they started reading the briefs of each plaintiff, they saw what I saw—no court would grant class action status to this group of plaintiffs. Too many different issues, no commonality or typicality. They petitioned the court for leave. In other words, they wanted out in a big way but needed the court's permission to opt out. The court excused them from the class action case that Goldberg and Gage was pursuing but made them take about fifteen plaintiffs with them to represent from that original case. I believe that the court gave Wasserman, Comden & Casselman their pick of the litter. I think they allowed them to cherry-pick which litigants they wanted to keep for themselves.

I say that because not too long after this media event and them asking the court for leave, I received a call from David Casselman of that firm who told me on the phone that he had been personally reviewing the files of cases they were going to take with them when they were dismissed from this case and he thought, out of all the cases he reviewed, I had one of the best cases and one of the worst cases of retaliation he had ever seen. I met with him to discuss the details of his firm taking over my case. It was the usual one-third spilt if it settles out of court and forty percent if we win at trial. This is called taking a case on a contingency basis and is about the only way (besides pro bono) to get an attorney to take your case with no per diem or retainer paid upfront. Good attorneys are in the $600 to $800 an hour range plus incidentals. So the law firm of Wasserman, Comden & Casselman chose their fifteen or so plaintiffs and were dismissed by the court from the original Goldberg and Gage lawsuit. So now the firm of Wasserman, Comden & Casselman had fifteen LAPD cases that they now had to represent as fifteen separate lawsuits. I didn't track those that stayed with Goldberg and Gage but from what I heard through my contacts in the police union, it didn't work out so well. The case, as I expected, was denied class action status. It fell apart. I cannot say for sure because of the confidential nature of these litigations but I did hear of some accusations of Goldberg and Gage dropping some clients or even being abandoned. I don't know for sure. However, I did talk to two of the plaintiffs that were colleagues of mine years later and they told me their cases were either dropped or thrown out.

Even though these cases with myself and about fourteen other police officers was not a class action and instead was a collective action, David Casselman wasn't stupid. He knew it would save a lot of time and money to approach the Los Angeles City Attorney's Office with one deal involving all plaintiffs. The cost of time and energy pursuing and defending fifteen different law suits would be millions. This is especially true when you consider that the Los Angeles City Attorney's Office, charged with defending these suits, outsourced many of its legal responsibilities to such prestigious law firms such as O'Melveny & Myers LLP. This firm has approximately eight hundred lawyers in sixteen offices worldwide. They are in the "The American Lawyer's" ranking of the nation's most well-rounded law firms. I had a friend who was a former federal prosecutor who, after about five years working for the federal government, left and joined the law firm of O'Melveny and Myers making approximately $200,000 a year to start.

Of course I didn't have privilege to what the other fourteen clients wanted as part of their settlement with the City of Los Angeles. To me, it wasn't about just money. My reputation was important to me. So was a career path with mobility into management. I desperately wanted my sergeant and detective promotions that I had already earned several times over the last eight years. My thinking was such that with my education, experience, and a clean record, I could eventually move into management. Considering at the time of the litigation that I had five college degrees (eventually to become seven), twenty-two years of law enforcement experience at the federal, county and municipal level, and no citizen complaints; the remedy of this lawsuit should, if agreed to, put me back on track to management. So it wasn't all about money but my reputation as well. About a year into the lawsuit, I started getting a sense of frustration from my attorney David Casselman. What I didn't know was that by around October of 2002, every one of the other fourteen plaintiffs in the lawsuit Casselman was handling had agreed to terms with the City of Los Angeles except me. Everyone wanted money but I wanted my clean record and reputation back.

The LAPD was at the time a strong, ten-thousand-sworn-member department. It was big enough that you could maybe take an interview for promotion with a panel that didn't know you and hadn't been given disparaging information about you ahead of time. So all they could judge you by was your personnel record and your oral interview scores. I was very good at taking oral interviews and always did quite well. The city's first offer to me was $400,000. I countered with an offer of $300,000 and them removing or expunging three false complaints out of my personnel package. I also asked for my promotion to sergeant or detective back. I even offered to retire in return for my promotion and pension and a "clean package." I now had fifteen years on with LAPD and my pension vested at ten years. If I could get out of that organization as a sergeant with a clean record, it would open up a lot of opportunities for me. LAPD is so big that a sergeant sitting in as a watch commander of just one of the twenty different patrol divisions on just one shift could have thirty or forty police officers under his or her supervision. I had seen LAPD sergeants make chief of police once retired at other law enforcement organizations. After about two months of negotiating with the City of Los Angeles the promotion and retirement deal came off of the table. I forget why. They probably wanted to continue retaliating against me and eventually get me terminated or hope I commit suicide like many officers had after going through similar persecution as I had. In several cases, I think, in my opinion, there could be prima facie evidence for negligent homicide or even manslaughter. At the minimum, a civil case for wrongful death should have been brought by the union on behalf of the survivors of officers that were pushed over the edge by the LAPD managerial hegemony and retaliatory machine. Some died from the bombardment of stress after years of willful retaliation that came in many forms. Some caved under pressure after their lives were ruined and killed themselves.

I know of one particular officer that was actually carried out by ambulance from an LAPD station because he kept being put at the front desk as punishment because he challenged their scrutiny of his use of his sick time. They knew his blood pressure was through the roof. They knew his injuries were real. However, they kept retaliating against him and they kept putting him back at the front desk despite pleas from him, me, and a supervisor not to do it. I knew this officer well. He was a devout Christian like me and we even boxed together and became friends. We worked the front desk together so I could see the effects the department was having on his health and they knew it. He was found late one night dead on his couch by one of his young children. Due to his prior history of high blood pressure and heart problems and stress, it was ruled a natural death. No one ever found out about the empty bottle of pills discovered by a supervisor at the scene and removed from the scene. You see, suicides often void a life insurance policy. This officer had young children and a wife. The sergeant that removed these pills took a chance at losing his career in order to allow the officer's family from avoiding certain financial collapse. I consider him a hero.

Retaliation doesn't always come in the form of death. A friend of mine who I went through the LAPD Academy with was unfortunate enough to be assigned to the now infamous Rampart Division around the time Rafael Perez was allegedly planting guns on arrestees and stealing narcotics from the LAPD evidence room. I hadn't seen him for several years after the Rampart incident. I ran into him several years later and he related to me the following story. Chief Bernard Parks was so obsessed with showing transparency after the Rampart scandal. Perez, in order to get a plea deal and better sentence, agreed to implicate what he claimed was a "widespread police misconduct" of other officers. This web spun by Perez eventually included seventy LAPD officers and supervisors. One of them was my friend. He was charged with several counts of misconduct including criminal and civil charges. Normally, police departments in California must abide by a one-year statute of limitations when investigating an employee. According to the Peace Officers Procedural Bill of Rights Act (G.C. § 3300-3312), law enforcement organizations have a one-year statute of limitations for the completion of an investigation and notification to an employee of proposed disciplinary action. Specifically, G.C. §3304 (d) states that: "except as provided in this subdivision and subdivision (g), no punitive action, ... shall be undertaken for any act, omission, or other allegation of misconduct if the investigation of the allegation is not completed within one-year of the public agency's discovery by a person authorized to initiate an investigation of the allegation of an act, omission, or other misconduct." However, there are exceptions to the one-year statute of limitations which the prosecutors and Internal Affairs Investigator took advantage of during the Rampart Investigation: 1. if the alleged misconduct is also the subject of a criminal investigation or criminal prosecution; 2. if the officer waives the one-year time period in writing; 3. if the investigation is multi-jurisdictional in nature and requires a reasonable extension for coordination of the involved agencies; 4. if more than one employee is involved in the investigation and a reasonable extension of time is needed; 5. if the investigation involves an employee who is incapacitated or otherwise unavailable; 6. if the investigation involves a matter in civil litigation where the officer is named as a party defendant; 7. if the investigation involves a complainant who is a criminal defendant, during the period of the defendant's criminal investigation and/or prosecution; and 8. if the investigation involves an allegation of Worker's Compensation fraud on the part of the officer. Since there were criminal and civil investigations going on as part of the Rampart investigations, the statute was tolled for years—many years.

However, I insisted on getting rid of those three complaints which will give me a ten-year history of no complaints and even the couple of complaints I had in my first few years on LAPD were very minor slaps on the wrist and certainly nothing to hold me back. the city came back and said that it was impossible to seal a complaint of a police officer's record. The City Attorney's Office gave me a long speech of how they conferenced with the LAPD and were told that it was not logistically feasible. They also said that it would set a bad precedence that every time an officer was disciplined, he or she could point to my case and say they wanted their records of complaints sealed. Also, that by doing this, it didn't serve the best interest of the public who expect officers' histories to be transparent and accurate. I then countered with $200,000 and they agreed to seal the three complaints. It seems I found the city's cost of doing the impossible. For $100,000, they could now seal my complaint history and do everything a month ago they said was impossible. Money talks. However, the devil was in the details as they say and as I would later find out. As I stated earlier, I only found this out later but my attorney was under enormous pressure from his firm and from the City of Los Angeles who told him flat out that they would settle either all the cases (all sixteen including mine) or none. They never wanted this case from the beginning once they saw it would never make class action status. My case wouldn't settle because I was insistent on how I wanted my complaints to be sealed. I knew the city would try to pull some trickery. I quoted both the California Penal Code and Evidence Code on expunging and sealing of complaints. I even wrote in the language of the settlement draft that I forwarded to Casselman that besides being expunged or sealed, these complaints could never be used against me to show a pattern of misconduct. LAPD was infamous for taking two small complaints that were years apart and trying to show a pattern of misconduct and that you were an employee who didn't learn from his mistakes. This would justify their termination of you from something very small. They could not be used against me or even considered for promotional purposes or negative disciplinary proceedings. They could not be used against me during the penalty phase of any disciplinary hearing. I made sure that I covered all my bases when I wrote this provision of my settlement. I forwarded it to my attorney right around Thanksgiving of 2002. I told him that these terms were non-negotiable. I heard nothing from my attorney all the way through Christmas and it was near New Year's when I finally got a call from Him. He said, "Good news, Barry. Good news. The city has agreed to everything you wanted." I said "Everything?" He answered in the affirmative and said he was looking at the city's proposal to me and had read it. I was both surprised and a little quizzical. Why all of a sudden would the city give up on an issue that they were so ardent against, especially when I presented it in the form I wanted with the Penal Code and Evidence Code as examples? It was because they thought they could slip something by me. When I cut them off by preempting them with this specific language of my proposal, they knew they couldn't pull one over on me. Why didn't they change their minds and why was my attorney calling me on December 30th insisting on signing the settlement right away? What I didn't know at the time was that my own lawyer became complicit with the city for his own good. He sold me out. He knew fully well what I wanted in the agreement. We had fought about it when the city refused to agree to terms I had insisted on. I had wrote to him the exact language I wanted. I had discussed it with him with a deputy city attorney in the room! He told me that he was under a deadline of the New Year's to get the deal done and he was just going to fax me over the signature page of the settlement agreement and all I would have to do is sign it and fax it back. He would FedEx me a copy of the agreement once all parties had signed. Big mistake on my part to acquiesce.

When I eventually got a copy of the settlement, I realized that I had been cheated. The agreement just said that my complaints would be removed from my personnel package but the original face sheet of the complaint forms would be left in my package for everyone to see! Every promotion board, disciplinary board, prospective employers, everyone could see the face sheet and know of the complaints. They couldn't read the actual complaints which was worse. If you took the time to read the actual complaints, the average person could see how ubiquitous they were. I immediately call my attorney and complained and he said that he was assured by the City Attorney's Office that this language would take care of all the concerns I had. I knew it wouldn't. I made the mistake of trusting my attorney and only found out later that he was complicit it this deal. I was told by two different individuals, one a former member of the Los Angeles City Attorney's Office and another who used to work for LAPD Risk Management Department of this skullduggery. I was told that the City Attorney's Office, and I am quoting this individual now, "put a gun to the head of your attorney." Now I don't obviously mean this literally but figuratively. My lawyers firm wanted desperately to get rid of these cases (including mine) from the beginning, but the judge made his firm take these cases. They wanted out. They had invested way too much money and time into the case. I was the last holdout. Casselman didn't want this on his resume. So he lied to me and committed several violations of the California State Bar Act and the Business and Professional Code. At least in my opinion and based on the evidence I discovered, this was the case. Years later when LAPD was trying yet again to terminate me, I went to him and asked him to draft a letter of intent showing that the original intent of the agreement was that it was not supposed to be used in promotional or discipline hearings—especially in an attempt to show patterns of misconduct. When I told what I was going through, I could tell that he felt bad about what he did. He made some statements to me that were part admission, part apology but he agreed to write the letter which in the end made no difference. I did do one smart thing however. It seems like a lot of money splitting six million dollars with fifteen other police officers but I knew after attorney's fees and taxes and a new tax bracket, I would end up with peanuts. So I put my law school education to work and began to do some legal research on tax exempt settlements. I researched and found a federal tax code consistent with the Internal Revenue Policy. I found a section that makes a settlement or jury award non-taxable if it says in the settlement documents that the award is for non-economical damages. So in my last draft of my settlement documents that I had given to my attorney to pass on to the Deputy City Attorney handling my case, I had written as part of the legal (money) settlement, "$200,000 to be paid to Barry Brooks as non-economical damages." They never caught it. So I didn't report it as income the following year's tax return. However, I knew that the LAPD would be calling the IRS to try notify them and to see if they could get me audited to further add stress to my life. Sure enough, they did. I got notification in June of 2004 by way of a very threatening letter. The Internal Revenue Service (having been tipped off by LAPD) wanted an immediate $80,000 plus penalties that would accrue every day. I sent a copy of the agreement that contained the wording "non-economical damages" and the federal tax code and a copy of their own regulations. I got back what I like to call a "you were right" letter, a *mea culpa* which is the closest I ever got to getting an apology from the Internal Revenue Service. Score one for the working man.

My last semester in law school I had applied and was accepted into the Los Angeles District Attorney's Office as an intern. This is a very prestigious and hard to get into internship. Many of their eventual deputy district attorneys are hired from their internship program. I was hired and brought on board and I was scheduled to go through the five-day prosecutor's school. I was assigned to LAX Courthouse, Division 142. Ironically, I had worked Pacific Division when they built this courthouse and a lot of my arrestees ended up being arraigned there and I testified there in criminal proceedings quite a lot. I was still assigned to Pacific Division of LAPD when I was assigned to division 142. I thought it would be kind of awkward to get up in front of a judge during the plea process and tell the judge that this guy is guilty and I know this because I arrested him. Probably wouldn't go over very well. So just when some things are going well, like this internship, along came LAPD to ruin it. Word got out that I had been recruited into the District Attorney's Office. I don't know who but I ran into officers and detectives all the time starting in the first week I was there which was mostly observation at the time. I was called into Steve, the Supervising Deputy's office, on my second week there. He said he had to let me go. I inquired why. He said that the LAPD had informed him that I had a Brady letter in my personnel package and with that in my file, I couldn't be an officer of the court.

This all began with an old but famous case called Brady vs. Maryland. The Supreme Court held in that case that withholding exculpatory evidence violates due process "where the evidence is material either to guilt or to punishment." The court determined that under Maryland state law the withheld evidence could not have exculpated the defendant but was material to the level of punishment he would be given. Modernly, a defendant's request for Brady disclosure refers to the holding of the Brady case, and the numerous state and federal cases that interpret its requirement that the prosecution disclose material exculpatory evidence to the defense. Exculpatory evidence is "material" if "there is a reasonable probability that his conviction or sentence would have been different had these materials been disclosed." Brady evidence includes statements of witnesses or physical evidence that conflicts with the prosecution's witnesses and evidence that could allow the defense to impeach the credibility of a prosecution witness. Police officers who have been dishonest are sometimes referred to as "Brady cops." Because of the Brady ruling, prosecutors are required to notify defendants and their attorneys whenever a law enforcement official involved in their case has a sustained record for knowingly lying in an official capacity. So all of a sudden, in the late 1990s, LAPD found a new way to mess with officers they didn't like. They would accuse you of some type of falsehood or lying or misleading because almost anything can be determined to be misleading. It is very subjective. Then they would issue you a Brady letter which was, once again, a kiss of death. It meant you were not trustworthy. Now, with a Brady letter in your personnel file, you cannot work the field as a police officer because if you work the field, you are going to make arrests and if you make arrests, you are going to be subpoenaed to testify. Then a defense attorney can file a pitches-motion to review your file and find your Brady letter and discredit and impeach you on the stand and essentially assassinate your character. This, by the way, could happened to you even if you were just accused of making some type of misleading statement or falsehood. It could take years, like Rampart, to investigate an allegation of administrative misconduct since the LAPD could toll the one-year statute of investigation under the Police Officers Bill of Rights for many things. This is not even considering the fact that you can never count on getting justice at an LAPD disciplinary hearing as I think I have established a prima facie case for.

So officers like me who received Brady letters were deskbound and could not be promoted. We were looked at by LAPD management as scum, proven or unproven. The net was cast wide for any accusation of misconduct involving an ounce of what could be perceived as deception. It was a new and very powerful weapon in the arsenal of Internal Affairs and ultimately LAPD management. So what did I do to earn a Brady letter? Back to my meeting with Steve Sobel at the District Attorney's Office. So after being notified by Sobel that LAPD had given me a Brady letter for which I was in shock because as far as I knew I was not under investigation for any misconduct and hadn't lied about anything. He left the office for a moment and I looked at the notification from LAPD and on the bottom of the page was the fax number it was sent from. It was from an old enemy. When I came back to work at Pacific Division a few days later, I was served with both a complaint and a Brady letter. It seems that one of the command staff officers sitting on my detective promotion oral interview board a few months earlier had accused me of lying to the board during my detective interview. He said I "misrepresented" myself as a police officer III instead of a police officer II. I did mention to the board several positive things that had recently happened in my life and career including just being chosen as the newest police officer III by my captain at Pacific Division. This was true. What I didn't know was that Captain K, who had promoted from commanding officer of Pacific Division to be the west bureau commander and was now my captain's boss. She overturned my promotion or more technically my pay grade advancement to police officer III. This lieutenant who sat on my detective promotional board was good friends with the commander and so was doing her a favor by filing this complaint against me, stopping my paygrade advancement, my promotion to detective, and getting me kicked out of the District Attorney's Office as well as the Brady letter. The Civil Service Commission had the jurisdiction to investigate my oral interview. They completed a thorough investigation and found no evidence of misconduct. Of course that wasn't good enough for LAPD because they "hold officers to a higher standard," which is their way of keeping an investigation going when an outside entity has found no evidence of the charge of misconduct. Eventually, at the end of 2003, after the union filed a lawsuit and settlement agreements ensued, I was given a five-figure settlement and the letter was removed from my personnel package. However, the damage was done. I had lost out on a once in a life time opportunity with the District Attorney's Office. Good thing I have God on my side.

The Attack on My Family

◆ ◆ ◆ ◆ ◆ ◆

You would think it is bad enough that the Los Angeles Police Department came after me. You would think that it would be enough that they had pretty much ruined my career, sabotaged my health (infra), and had not let up for about eight to nine years by this time. You would be wrong. They went after my wife as well. In 2004, despite her seeing first-hand everything the LAPD did to me, my wife wanted to join the LAPD. Ever since she was a little kid, she wanted to become a police officer. Her father wouldn't let her move out of the house until she was married or went off to college where he couldn't control her. He sure wasn't going to let her become a police officer or deputy. In fact, he tried to marry her off when she was eighteen. She was sent back to their home country of Egypt and had suitors lined up to marry her. She didn't know of course, thinking this was a get to know some of your distant relatives' trip. Once she found out, she immediately rebuffed that idea and came back to Los Angeles. Her culture is very paternalistic and very patriarchic. The father is in charge and the women must remain virgins until they are married. It is ironic that her parents brought her to America when she was two years old to give her a better life but then when she became a teenager and Americanized, tried to imprison her much like the Muslims do. When she was twenty-one years old, she was traveling through Europe with her friend Deanna because Deanna's mother lived in London. Her father was so afraid of her losing her virginity and his control over her that in order to get her back to Los Angeles, he offered to buy her a store.

He bought her a vintage clothing store just two blocks off the beach in Venice. She agreed and signed a seven-year lease in 1990. A few years later, she would be burglarized and call the police and at the time I was working Venice Beach as a police officer and got the call. And so we met. Almost twenty-five years later, we have been married for over twenty-two years and have four children together. Who says crime doesn't pay?

However, getting back to the LAPD, right around 2004, we had been married for a decade and her vintage clothing store had now been closed since 1997. She worked at Rite-Aid as an assistant manager in order to help us qualify for the mortgage on the new house that God had blessed us with. A few years later, she had taken a job as a medical claims examiner with the Department of Veterans Affairs. However, by 2004 she wanted to fulfill her dream of going into law enforcement. So she passed the LAPD written exam and I coached her on her oral interview panel and helped her get into the police academy. We knew that we would have to try to shield her from her connection to me—LAPD's *persona non grata*. We thought about putting her in the academy under her maiden name but she had to go under her legal name. Well they knew who she was the very first day of the police academy. In fact, they changed her academy class and assigned her to a class in which the drill instructor was the son of a female LAPD captain that I had successfully sued—Sharon Buck. It didn't take long for him to go to work on her. They walked in to the academy class the first day and yelled "Who use to work for the Veterans Affairs Office?" Knowing they were trying to pick on her and intimidate her in front of her classmates, she stayed silent. Her first week in the academy, they would single her out, deny her bathroom privileges, and just take every chance to berate her and embarrass her. By the end of the first week in the academy, I got a phone call from her and she was crying. She told me that they had locked her into a room and denied her food, water, and bathroom privileges. They threatened her that unless she signed a voluntary agreement to quit the department, they were going to make her life a living hell. She had snuck out of the room and got her cell phone to call me. I was incensed and my first instinct was to drive down to the academy and knock some people out. I knew this wouldn't end well and would give them the ammunition they needed to terminate me which is what I think they were baiting me in for. Instead, I called the Los Angeles Police Protective League—my union—and reported to them what had happened. I discussed the situation with League Director Paul Webber. He called down to the commanding officer, Captain Diaz, another command staff officer who would later be instrumental in trying to terminate me. I have to give Paul Webber credit. He threatened to come down there and file false imprisonment charges on everyone from the captain down. It worked and she was let go. We filed a personnel complaint against several of the cadre which was allegedly investigated without even interviewing me or my wife and it was dismissed. No one was held accountable.

My children and my home were not off limits either. One day a young boy started showing up in the neighborhood. He was about thirteen years old and befriended my son who at the time was about eight years old. I saw this kid talking with my son and I decided to find out who he was. He was very evasive. "I live around here" and "I am staying at a friend's house" were the responses I got from him. He quickly befriended my son and asked him if he had ever done drugs and if he would like to try some. My son was raised right and said no. Then he started asking a lot of questions about me. He asked my son what type of work does your father do and after my son told him I was a cop, he asked him where I keep my guns. I didn't find this part out until later. My son told him that I keep a gun locked in the console of my personal vehicle which was normally parked in the garage. However, my wife and I were having some construction done on the garage and had been parking our cars in the driveway. I had also been seeing an unmarked police car, a Ford Crown Vic, around the neighborhood and parked down the street on a few occasions. They are not hard to spot with the antenna in the back and the exempt license plate on the back. That night my handgun was stolen out of my console. I had the local police department (not LAPD) conduct an investigation. They determined that the break in was done with a "slim Jim" device used mainly by professionals. Naturally, I reported the theft to my LAPD supervisors as required.

This, however, was my personal handgun and not the department's. So far, the event didn't look suspicious although there were some strange circumstances surrounding the theft of my handgun. It soon got even stranger. A few weeks went by and my wife and I were heading up to California Wine country for a couple of days to get away. We were driving and reached Ventura County when I received one of the strangest phone calls I had ever gotten. My cell phone rang and it was my commanding officer's adjutant. He ordered me back to my residence in Orange County (now about one hundred miles away) and to await further orders. Now I was on a couple of days off from work and I argued that point judiciously. However, after being threatened with a charge of insubordination, which they cannot legally do but would, I made the decision to turn around and fully cooperate. My wife and I were full of apprehension. What were they trying to do? There was always an ulterior motive with LAPD management. A simple task or request always was setting you up for something.

After a couple of hours, we made it back home. Parked in front of my home was what looked like that same undercover or take-home car as we called them that I had seen before. As I pulled into my driveway, I saw Detective Ventrano step out of his vehicle and walk toward me. Now I have known Detective Ventrano for a long time. He had investigated and assisted in the prosecution of a lot of crimes and arrests that I had made over the years. He was now a supervisory detective assigned to LAPD homicide, Pacific Division. I looked at him and said, "What's going on?" He told me that he was ordered by the commanding officer of Pacific Division to come search my garage and my car. I asked him why. He said he didn't know why he was ordered to my house and that he was under orders not to say anything to me. I asked him if he had a duly authorized search warrant. He said he did not have one but the commanding officer told him that this is an administrative search. *Administrative search?* I thought. Administrative searches are when the Police Department or any employer is allowed to search your desk, your locker or even computer because it belongs to the employer. You cannot search an employee's home on the guise of an administrative search. He told me that it wasn't coming from him but the commanding officer and that if I refused, I would be facing a Board of Rights disciplinary hearing which could include a penalty all the way up to termination of employment. So I acquiesced and let him know that I was allowing the search under threat of compulsion and not of my own free will and volition. I asked him why they sent him, a homicide detective, and not internal affairs or one of my area supervisors from Pacific Patrol Division. He said it was because he lived close by, in Huntington Beach. This was true. I had heard that he lived a few miles away. Still, for a homicide detective to show up at your front door with orders for an illegal search, who appeared to not want to be there was just beyond bizarre. Was this some type of retaliation for my lawsuits or other legal victories against the LAPD? My wife and I stood there for about an hour as Detective Ventrano search every inch of my garage and then tore my Tahoe apart. He took photos, wrote down notes, and made a few phone calls out of earshot. I did the best I could to keep an eye on him without getting in the way. If I had had a video camera, I would have videotaped the whole thing. Even though I knew him personally and generally trusted him, I didn't want him planting anything in my garage or car. Eventually, he called it quits. I asked him if he found what he was looking for. He just shrugged his shoulders and gave a half-hearted apology and he got in his car and left. It would take me a decade to find out what the modus operandi was behind the whole episode.

Fast forward to the autumn of 2015. I came home from teaching a constitutional law course at the university and had two messages on my home phone. The first one was from a gang officer from Torrance, California Police Department. Torrance is a large beach city near Los Angeles that has some violent gang elements in it. The second message was from a homicide detective also from Torrance Police Department. Both calls were to "LAPD Officer Barry Brooks" and were about my handgun that got stolen almost eight years earlier. I called back and spoke to the officer that had called me and the conversation went something like this: He was working a gang unit and arrested a gang member for armed robbery who had long-term ties to a gang in Los Angeles. The investigation revealed that my handgun may be tied to at least one homicide from a long time ago. They wanted to verify that I had made the police report with Cosa Mesa Police Department about eight years earlier. They had to call Costa Mesa Police Department due to the fact that my name, driver's license, and vehicle registration are all confidential due to being a police officer. Costa Mesa Police Department pulled up a copy of the stolen handgun report which had my phone number on it and were gave it to Torrance Police so they could contact me. Torrance Police also told me that they would have to hang on to the gun as evidence in order to prosecute the robbery and any other crimes, such as murder, that ballistics and other evidence could put the gun at the scene of a crime.

It all made sense now. My gun disappearing, the mysterious kid who got information from my son on my handgun's whereabouts, the illegal search of my garage and car. I believe that my gun was deliberately stolen by the direction of someone pretty high up within LAPD management. I also believe that they took the gun and allowed it to go out on to the street and into the hands of some very bad people—gangsters, murderers, Mexican mafia, etc. I think that they inexplicably were going to use the search of my vehicle and garage as either a ruse to put my handgun back after it had been used in a crime or they were looking for some personal object of mine like a piece of clothing or an identification to be left at the scene of a crime along with my handgun. Maybe since I was keeping such a close eye on the detective that he didn't feel comfortable putting the gun back in my car. Think about it. The Costa Mesa Police had already searched and fingerprinted my vehicle when my handgun was stolen. It wasn't stolen from my garage. So the detective would need access to my garage to look around and suddenly find it. It would look like I used the gun in a homicide and then lied about it being stolen to cover up the weapon or instrument of the crime. The alternative is plausible as well. If my gun was actually stolen as I had reported it and it was used in a crime, it wouldn't pose any legal jeopardy on me as they would have to put me at the scene of the crime as well. However, if something personal to me, something that had my DNA, fingerprints, or name on it was found at the scene along with my gun, then how would I explain that? Something went wrong with their plan and my handgun was either kept out on the street all those years or put back out years later maybe for some other nefarious purpose. Nothing else makes sense. In fact, during the time that my handgun was stolen from my car, my locker at the police station had been broken into. I came into work and the lock was cut off. No explanation. So I bought a new lock. Maybe they were looking for something personal to put me at the scene of a crime but I don't keep anything in my LAPD locker except uniforms and gear. Logically, what other explanation can there be for the circumstances surrounding the disappearance of my weapon? So it seems they weren't content with just ruining my reputation, demoting me six times, putting false complaints in my personnel file, denying me work permits, wreaking havoc with my work shifts, getting me thrown out of the District Attorney's Office, forcing my wife out of the LAPD Academy and other hostile acts—they wanted me in jail. I also wondered if Sergeant Arneson had something to do with this. He certainly had motive, even from behind bars. He had worked homicide and gangs and hand a lot of connections. His former girlfriend and captain of LAPD Internal Affairs had vowed to get even with me. His co-conspirator, Anthony Pelicano, allegedly had connections to the CIA and to the criminal underground. I guess I will probably never know this side of heaven.

The Prelude

❖ ✦ ✦ ✦ ❖

By 2005, against all odds and of course with God's help, I was still employed by the Los Angeles Police Department. They could not believe that I was still around despite what at this time had been ten years of attempts to get rid of me. They didn't like me because I was a fighter. So much so that I had dropped out of my PhD program and put myself through law school to learn how to fight back. They had filed five false complaints about me and I had had three sealed by court order (which they ignored) and two removed by successful petition of writ of mandamus. I had lost four promotions and three paygrade advancements but I had a class action lawsuit working its way through the legal system which would hopefully remedy this issue. I was starting to get a sense of hope that I might make it to 2008 so I could get my twenty years in and earn my service pension.

Then they tried a new tactic in trying to ruin me by saying that I was abusing my sick time. After Chief Bratton had been hired by the LAPD in 2002, he took a special interest in sick and light duty police officers. Although Chief Bratton wasn't around much, preferring to be hobnobbing in London, New York, and Washington DC, he made it known to the command staff of LAPD that he wanted to go after officers who he felt were abusing their sick time. The Los Angeles Police Department was kind of unique, at least from my perspective, in that when an officer got permanently injured, disfigured, or just plain limited in function, they did not pension them off. Most police departments would not keep an officer around if he could not be field-certified. That is, police work has requirements in the scope and job description which requires an officer to be able to handle field work. In laymen's terms, heavy lifting, repetitive squatting, bending, etc. When Chief Bratton joined the ranks of LAPD, approximately ten percent of LAPD officers were "light duty." That means that they were not physically fit to work a field assignment. LAPD placed these officers in position that most other police agencies would fill with civilian employees. The front desk is a good example of this. LAPD has twenty different geographical divisions and many substations that man the desks with police officers instead of volunteers or civilian employees. When Chief Bratton saw that approximately a thousand of his police officers were light duty, he became incensed. He wanted to get rid of them but due to California Labor codes (especially labor code 4850), Memorandums of Understanding, and established administrative laws, they could not pension them off. He made a unilateral decision that these officers were lazy and must be abusing the system. You see, if an officer became sick or hurt that was job-related such as being shot in the line of duty, then it would be deducted from his sick time bank. It took weeks and sometimes months for the City of Los Angeles Workman's Compensation fund to kick in. There was a long process of a supervisor turning in the proper paper work and then it went to the area work comp coordinator, LAPD medical liaison and eventually through the outside contracted workers Compensation Company such as Tristar or Firm Solutions. However, even in obvious cases such as an officer being hurt on the job while in uniform, the City of Los Angeles would often make you sue them to prove it was an injury on duty (IOD). My old partner, Darius Lee, got shot in the head by a barricaded suspect and luckily lived. He had to sue the City of Los Angeles for worker's compensation benefits and for his trouble, they gave him a four-day suspension. So on paper, to the bureaucrats, when they saw that you may have used one hundred hours of your sick time without realizing that you may have been seriously injured on the job, they would start a "sick file" on you. This included sending a supervisor to your home to door knock and see if you were really sick. Sometimes officers were at their physician's office or the pharmacy when the supervisor came by. There is nothing in policy or in the labor code that says you have to stay home when using a sick day. So a supervisor would make an entry into his supervisor's log that the officer who called in sick wasn't home.

Chief Bratton saw this as an issue of laziness and abuse. I don't think he fully understood that when officers are hurt on the job that it comes off the books as sick time at first before a conversion letter comes from the workman's compensation adjuster and you get credited back your sick time bank. I also don't think that he realized the willingness of the City of Los Angeles to keep police officers employed even if they could not and perhaps may never not ever become field certified during the rest of their careers. The origins of LAPD Workerman's Compensation Fraud Unit (WCFU) can be traced back to 1984 when, under Chief Daryl Gates, it was known as the Benefits Abuse Team (BAT). Many of the more tenured officers are familiar with what was more popularly known as the BAT Team. The BAT Team primarily utilized surveillance techniques on long-term injured on duty (IOD) and long-term sick employees suspected of abusing their medical benefits. The BAT Team was subsequently renamed the Claims Validation Unit (CVU). Both were organized within Medical Liaison Section to preserve the confidentiality of medical records. In 2004, the Workers' Compensation Reform Bill was passed and CVU was relocated to Professional Standards Bureau, Special Operations Division, (aka Internal Affairs) and renamed the WCFU. The insurance codes governing workers' compensation had markedly changed and medical information related to such claims were no longer protected by HIPPA when fraud was suspected. In fact, employers now have access to all medical records related to a work-related injury. Approximately $80 million is paid out every year to Department employees for IOD claims and therefore the department's workers' compensation system is a major budgetary expense for the city. One of the supposed cornerstones of WCFU's mission is to save money by exposing, investigating, and filing criminal and/or administrative cases involving such fraud. As department employees, we are entitled to receive the benefits and treatment necessary to return us to the way we were prior to our injuries or "made whole." Most officers should be commended for continuing to work with chronic pain from the rigors of police work. When they are unable to work full-duty, the department offers a very generous assortment of modified duty assignments and flexibility for physical therapy sessions.

Unfortunately, as I alluded to, Chief Bratton had a disdain for light duty or injured-on-duty (IOD) personnel. It is rumored that he doubled the amount of investigators on the benefit abuse team. One example of their overzealousness occurred around 2005. I was an employee representative at the time which means that when employees get accused of violating policy, then I can represent them during administrative interviews or boards. Officer Rollins had hurt his shoulder pretty badly and had corrective surgery to fix it. He hurt his shoulder at work so the injury was considered an on-duty injury. He came up to me in the hallway one day and asked for my advice. Recently, he had been at his son's Pop Warner football practice. He was still recovering from surgery and was in therapy for his shoulder but was on course to return to work in a few weeks. During the practice, he was just sitting on the sidelines. They were short a coach that day so the head coach asked him if he could toss the football around with some of the players. His shoulder felt comfortable enough to toss light throws back and forth to the players. Unfortunately for him, during the practice he got into an argument with another player's parents who knew he was an LAPD officer and reported him to internal affairs. He had been interviewed by internal affairs already and it seemed like a wash. A typical he said, she said situation. However, then internal affairs apparently found out the officer Rollins was off on IOD status when this incident occurred. He told me they wanted to re-interview him. He didn't know what to make of it. He didn't see the big picture—that they were out for blood. I pulled him aside and told him, "They want your job!" "What do you mean?" he said as he looked at me puzzled. As I explained to him what they were trying to do, he asked me to represent him. I had started to get a reputation as someone who took on the department and had been pretty successful. However, I knew he needed an attorney and someone that specialized in labor law. I directed him to make an appointment with the Los Angeles Police Protective League (LAPPL), our union, and get before the legal committee. The legal committee which met every other Tuesday could authorize the payment of legal counsel and resources that he would need to fight for his job. I saw him maybe one more time a month later and then never again. With ten thousand sworn police officers transferring in and out of divisions all the time, it was hard to keep track of people. Little did I know that the next sick time administrative complaint I would defend would be mine.

Perhaps taking his cue from Chief Bratton, my new commanding officer at Pacific Division was Captain Eisenburg. Captain Eisenburg was a golden boy. He made Captain in about fifteen years which is incredibly fast. He also had a background with the Federal Bureau of Investigation. He didn't like anyone that he felt was abusing their sick time privileges. By this time in my career, I had now injured my back severely after being followed home and run over in an ambush, had lung damage from having a chemical grenade thrown towards me by a domestic terrorist, had part of my stomach removed, new sphincter valve put in my stomach/diaphragm, had been treated for cancerous cells in my esophagus, torn my bicep, left elbow and other injuries and illnesses. By this point in time, the department had me working the front desk for up to twelve hours at a time with most of it standing. This caused tremendous pain and spasms in my back. I had been ignoring my surgeon's advice to have major back surgery and had a couple of epidurals to help with the pain. Wearing twenty pounds of gear each day didn't help either. My surgeon suggested to me to get a handicap placard. I thought this was ridiculous. He responded to me that I had two children and a wife who was now pregnant with our third child and how it might be easier to unload the entire family for example if we went to the mall or some place in which we might find ourselves parking a long ways away from the entrance. It made sense. I decided to go ahead with it convincing myself that I would not abuse it and only use it when necessary and when no one else needed it. As it turns out, Pacific Division repainted their back parking lot and put in one handicap spot next to the rear door of the station where officers parked and conducted ingress and egress of the station. So you had the two parking spots reserved for the two commanding officers of Pacific Division which at the time was Captain Eisenberg (Captain I of Pacific Patrol) and Captain Hayes (Captain III of Pacific Area). These, of course, were the best parking spots except for the handicap spot which by law they were required to place the closest to the back entrance.

It would be a little disingenuous of me to say that I started parking in the handicap spot because I really need to be that close to the rear entrance. At this point, I was about eleven years into my battle against LAPD management and I saw a little bit of an opportunity to stick their nose in it. I wanted show them that despite their best efforts I was still around. So I started parking in the newly created handicap parking spot next to Captain Eisenberg's parking spot. One day I was parking my car and he came in the lot and parked next to me in his assigned commanding officers spot. I waited for him to get out of his car and I got out of mine. I looked over at him and said, "Nice parking spot Captain but you got to be a VIP to get my spot." This, of course, was meant to be somewhat antagonistic. Not exactly very Christian-like but I had a moment of weakness. As I thought, it was successful. Captain Eisenberg immediately went to work and assigned sergeant White to investigate this incident. There was an enormous violation of my HIPPA rights when they gained access to my IOD and sick file from LAPD medical liaison and started to call and intimidate my surgeons and physicians into changing my medical records and status. I received a phone call from my thoracic surgeon, Dr. Maish from UCLA. Her nurse, Becky, said that she was getting intimidating calls from some LAPD sergeant telling her that she needed to turn over all of my medical records and that she needed to recant my medical limitations. Of course, she denied this request. After a few weeks, I was pulled into a meeting by my patrol lieutenant and handed a comment card. Comment cards were a form that was used by supervision and management that went into your local (divisional) personnel package. I was handed a comment card by the lieutenant directed from the captain and authored by Sergeant White. In essence, it stated that after a thorough and comprehensive review of all of my accumulated injuries and trauma over my career, that it was the captain's opinion that I did not merit the ability to use a handicap space. I looked up at the lieutenant and the sergeant after reading it and I said, "When did the captain graduate from medical school?" The comment cards were being used by LAPD management as a way to try to get around the formal discipline system which would require them to follow the Police Officers Bill of Rights and all of the procedural notice and due process required under the government and administrative codes.

Detective Tyler Izen, former President of the Los Angeles Police Protective League (LAPPL), expressed the exasperation of the abuse by LAPD management of these comment cards in an article he penned in the Blue Line (the LAPPL monthly newsletter) with the following comments: "Employee Comment Sheets, better known as comment cards, are designed to be used to document positive and negative conduct. The purpose is to either single out an individual for praise or to initiate corrective action before behavior deteriorates. However, we have recently seen the department issue comment cards to all sworn personnel on a watch to deal with a commanding officer's expectations. In our view, the wholesale issuance of comment cards violates the department's own guidelines on the issuance of comment sheets and a previous agreement between us that prohibits the mass issuance of canned language comment sheets. It bothers me that there are some in our command staff who believe that the mass issuance of comment sheets defining expectations is an effective method of communication. Everyone recognizes the need for commanding officers to clearly convey their expectations through and to subordinate employees. In fact, former US Secretary of State General Colin Powell said, 'Successful leaders know how to define their mission, convey it to their subordinates and ensure they have the right tools and training needed to get the job done.' While General Powell didn't specifically mention comment sheets, he did start the sentence with the word "successful." I believe it is as important to me as it is to the Chief of Police that you are efficiently and effectively fulfilling the mission of the Los Angeles Police Department. I firmly believe your life is far more fulfilling and complete when, in addition to receiving compensation and recognition, you are proud of the work you do. I

BARRY Q. BROOKS J.D.

am hopeful, if not naïve, that I have the support of more command officers than not, and can encourage and cajole department leadership to more effectively communicate their expectations than with a comment sheet that is issued to an entire unit, section, or division. In the meantime, it is important for officers who receive cookie-cutter comment cards to contact the league. Our current Memorandum of Understanding allows for officers to respond to Employee Comment Sheets using a 15.7 within thirty days of the initial review. Any employee response shall be attached to the Employee Comment Sheet (Manual Section 3/760.13). Note: If the Employee Comment Sheet is subsequently attached to a Standards Based Assessment, the employee shall have the right to contest such use via the grievance procedure. However, the Employee Comment Sheet itself will not be invalidated, destroyed or otherwise removed from the employee's personnel package unless such treatment is specifically directed by an arbitrator through arbitration of the Standards Based Assessment."

The above comment encapsulates the abuse of these comment cards by LAPD management and it was a back door way of putting something negative in in officer's personnel package without going through the formal system of protections offered by the California Police Officers Bill of Rights. It wasn't a big deal in and of itself but I wanted to beat them at their own game. I had thirty days to respond to the comment card in writing as per the current Memorandum of Understanding (MOU). I went to work gathering all of my seventeen years' worth of documented injuries, medical reports, LAPD awards for heroism I had received for being injured in the line of duty, the California Department of Motor Vehicles permit to use handicap parking, and the letter from a very renowned physician who had signed off on it. I complete a 15.7 employee's report that was two pages in length that outlined all of the violations of federal, state, municipal and LAPD policy that the captain had violated with this comment card regarding my injuries. I submitted my reply to the captain's adjutant who forwarded up to the captain. I didn't hear anything for several months. Obviously the captain knew that he couldn't win. He was a police captain making a medical decision. I think he realized that he had laid the ground for an Americans with Disability Act claim against him which can be up to $25,000 per violation. I know a lot of time and effort were put into this investigation to prove that I did not somehow medically qualify to have handicap parking privileges. I had friends at LAPD Medical Liaison and other places that would tell me about these inquiries, albeit illegal ones, made by the captain and his designates. So the captain had spent six months and countless hours using up taxpayer funds and LAPD employees and tried to coerce physicians and others to opine that there was absolutely nothing physically wrong with me and therefore he could go after me for medical fraud. His efforts failed. So then he tried a new tactic.

About six months went by and I thought the matter was over. Then I was on a day off in my home and received a phone call from Sergeant Brian Whitten who was the captain's adjutant. As I believe that I have demonstrated, I have had my share of shocking and surprising phone calls from the LAPD. This one ranks up there near the top with them all. I received a phone call from Sergeant White in which he stated the following (paraphrased), "We've done an exhaustive review of all your medical history and we have come to the conclusion that you are no longer physically fit to be a Los Angeles Police Officer." "What are you talking about?" I said. They had spent six months trying and failing to prove that my injuries were so slight that I was not qualified to possess a handicap placard. Sergeant Whitten stated further, "You have been 'decertified' as a police officer and tomorrow you will get a phone call from personnel division. They are going to reassign you as a parking officer (meter maid)." Hard to believe even from one of the most administratively corrupt law enforcement institutions in America that they would do a complete one hundred and eighty degree turn from saying I wasn't injured to now saying that I am too injured to perform the functions of a police officer. I was 270 lbs. at 12% body fat and could bench, squat and dead lift 500 lbs. for each lift. Hardly unable to perform my duties. What incredible hypocrisy. I had to admit, this was yet another unique method they were trying to pull to get rid of me. They were getting inventive and quite confident in themselves. I would make them pay. I don't think they realized that I was full-duty.

After all, how can you be full-duty but still injured enough to be able to qualify for handicap status? First, I was working the desk not out of reason of being injured but because I was being punished from the prior administration. Yes, I had a lot of permanent injuries over my career but I kept myself full-duty for two reasons. First, I was still hoping to be promoted by a victory in court which would soon be decided. I had already successfully competed and was supposed to be promoted to sergeant twice, to detective twice and to corporal (P-III) several times. The Los Angeles Police Protective League (LAPPL) had financed the Brown-Gregson lawsuit in which I was a part of. They were trying to resolve these chaotic Boards of Inquiry kangaroo courts and settle on an equitable remedy which I hoped would be my long awaited promotion(s). You cannot promote within the ranks of LAPD if you are not full-duty or had an open complaint against you. The other reason that I stayed field ready was pride. During this time of punishment being inside and on the desk which is one of the worst and most stressful jobs on the department, I got an occasional glimpse of the streets. A new watch commander or someone on loan not knowing I was in the penalty box would let me out on the streets and even act as a training officer since I had a lot more experience than many of the training officers (P-III) at Pacific Division.

I responded to the attempt to decertify me quickly and forcefully. I called the union, my attorney, the civil service commission, medical liaison and just about anyone else I could think of. It was the quickest withdrawal of a decision I had ever seen by an LAPD command staff officer. The following day, just twenty-four hours later, I received a call from the captain's adjutant in a very sheepish voice telling me that it was all a misunderstanding. Nevertheless, this captain continued the pattern and practice of retaliation by filing three comment cards against me for sick time abuse and overtime issues. I grieved them and won two out of three of these grievances in which the Captain was caught falsifying an overtime slip (greenie) of mine. However, he was never charged. It did prove to be somewhat cathartic in nature.

Two Weddings and a Funeral

✦✦✦✦✦

The attempt to end my police career by filing numerous false complaints against by June of 2007 had failed. Their plan to decertify me as a police officer had failed. Their failing to allow me to promote to sergeant and detective several times had failed. I could sense their desperation. They had made it very clear that if they could not get rid of me then they were going to keep me from promoting and just keep filing false complaints against me until I quit or until they would seize an opportunity to terminate me. However, once again, after several years of defeats, I was looking at some promising victories. I think what they also hoped for was that I would have a heart attack and die. I don't say this lightly but I have seen this before. They had killed my friend Rob by repeatedly putting him on the most stressful place an officer could work—the front desk. Even after he was taken away by ambulance from the front desk when his blood pressure went to 210/110, they still kept putting him on the desk because he fought management. They felt that Rob was abusing his sick time when in fact, he was only using it as an attempt to heal from the stress they kept creating for him. It did eventually cost him his life. I know of several other officers who took their own lives after going through the stress the department put them through. I myself had recently just had major surgery to fix Barret's esophagus, hiatal hernia, and had a new stomach valve put in. In short, the stress from what the LAPD had put me through had caused severe damage to my intestinal tract, stomach, and gastro system. The stress had caused my liver to pump pure bile into my stomach to compensate for the protease pump inhibitors given to me by my physician after I started throwing up blood. The acid and bile ate my stomach valve that opens and closes to let food into the stomach but keep acid from coming up into the esophagus. So at night, when I slept, the acid would come up my esophagus, cause precancerous cells and then I would swallow from reflux and the acid would irritate my lungs making it difficult to breathe. I was on a nebulizer for quite a while until I finally had to have surgery and have a valve from a cadaver put into my stomach and have the hiatal hernia surgically corrected. I was also breaking out in hives from the stress and some of my hair was falling out.

Nevertheless, Captain Eisenberg's solution was to get rid of me. LAPD was now under a federal consent decree and not doing well. They created a new detail to assist with getting LAPD past the federal consent decree called the Quality Assurance Achievement Cadre or QAAC for short. So the good captain saw a chance to get rid of me and "loaned" me to the QAAC team. My new job was to report each day to a different division and conduct spot checks of arrest reports, juvenile logs, etc. to make sure that policy was being adhered to. For me, and I think they knew this, it was the worst job in the world being a paper pusher. I bit the bullet and did the best job I could waiting for equitable relief from my pending lawsuit in which I was seeking both promotions to sergeant and to detective.

In September of 2007, my lawsuit was successfully settled and part of the settlement was to have fair administrative hearings to merit promotion. These new administrative hearings were supposed to be a slam dunk and unless major misconduct had happened since the settlement, would almost certainly be granted. There were forty of us plaintiffs, police officers that had been victims of the department's kangaroo court also known as the Boards of Inquiry that were used to halt promotions for political purposes without any due process at all. As discussed, these were supposed to be hearings that were very favorable to the officer as stipulated by the settlement. Therefore, the department was not going to call any adverse witnesses during these proceedings and give only cursory challenges to personnel complaints made against an officer since the lawsuit started. I had not had a sustained complaint in a long time so I knew this wasn't an issue. I received a phone called from my union representative from the Los Angeles Police Protective League, John Mumma. I have said this and I will continue to say this through this book, I received another eye opening phone call. John told me that out of the forty appeals the department was going to give to every defendant involved in the lawsuit, I was the only person that the department was going to call adverse witnesses against. Just me. The other thirty-nine officers would not have the department bringing in adverse witnesses. On top of this, Mumma asked me the following question verbatim, "What the fuck did you ever do to Lieutenant Ron Spicer?" I told him that I had never heard of him although I knew he worked Employee Relations along with my old boss whose boyfriend went to prison in part because of the information I provided to internal affairs. Mumma told me that Lieutenant Spicer had told him directly that he would make sure that I never promoted within the LAPD. The scary part was that it was Employee Relations that was overseeing these new appeals that would decide my fate to promote to both sergeant and detective. The department didn't stop there. Sergeant Lovitt, the department's advocate and the one I would be facing as the departments prosecutor during my appeal hearings, tried to use three former complaints against me that had been sealedas part of my lawsuit settlement three years earlier. They were not to ever be used for promotion purposed in a negative manner or to show a pattern of misconduct in a Board of Rights. I tried to get Deputy Chief Perez to intervene but he refused.

At this point, it almost became humorous. The first adverse witness they were going to call against me was Captain John Incontro. I was told that he was going to say "If Barry Brooks ever promotes to sergeant, I will quit the Department." Strong words. Problem is that I never worked for the man. He was my captain at Pacific Division for several months before he moved on. However, he was there at a time in which I was recovering from major surgery and was at home recovering. Thus, I had never directly worked for the man. I couldn't even tell you what he looked like. Mumma and I challenged Incontro's appearance at my two promotional appeals boards and were successful. Next, the department pulled Captain Jeri Weinstein out of its hat. If you remember, it was she who swore revenge on me after I was involved in the investigation that put her boyfriend in prison for eleven years. So that fair right? A hearing for two promotions which I had now waited twelve years for was going to be put in the hands of a woman who had told me and others that she was out for vengeance against me. Nothing inherently unfair there. Especially since I was the only officer out of forty that the department was going to call adverse witnesses against. Thanks to John Mumma, he was able to get Weinstein tossed out of the proceedings. In a last ditch effort to bring some adverse witness against me during my two appeals for sergeant and detective, the department pulled Margaret Taylor out of the hat. She was a civilian that was in charge of the time keeping and overtime process at Pacific Division. I had recently filed a complaint against her because she unilaterally refused to pay me for overtime worked and docked my pay without reason. Later, I was told that she was transferred and under investigation for fraud and theft of çity money by people I know at the Los Angeles Police Protective League. We were successful in stopping all these adverse witnesses. On December 2, 2007, after attending my two promotional hearings I was told by John Mumma that I had prevailed on both my appeals for sergeant and detective. The chief of police had signed off on both promotions. Now I would be put on the promotion transfer list and be promoted within the next six months. I call these victories my two "weddings" because it almost seemed like LAPD and myself had reconciliation, much like a bad marriage that was headed for divorce before both parties realized they had more to lose than gain. Things were definitely looking up. However, soon there would be a funeral.

The very same day that I had received the good news of being the first employee in LAPD history to be promoted twice in one day (sergeant and detective), I received yet another infamous phone call from my boss over at the QAAC team, Commander Louis Gray. He told me that I was the subject of a complaint and that it was being sent over to Internal Affairs Group to be investigated. I was baffled. I knew that I had done nothing wrong. It seems that in desperation, those who were not going to allow me to get promoted decided to go through over one thousand audits that I had completed as a member of the audit (QAAC) team and found two mistakes. This was apparently enough to charge me with neglect of duty. I spent the first four months of 2008 trying to adjudicate the complaint as month after month went by and my two promotions I won were starting to be seen in the rear view mirror. The department tried a new tactic in stealing my duty weapon and then conducting an illegal search on my car and my garage without a search warrant which I have already discussed. As I posited, I believe they were trying to pin a murder on me or place the weapon back in my garage and say I lied about it and terminate me. Termination or prison. Either way they got the result they wanted. When the theft of my handgun didn't work, the department had to try another tactic.

I had been interviewed at my attorney David Winslow's office on the audit complaint in March. Now in April, I was charged by Captain Eisenberg with insubordination for being interviewed on a day off instead of on a regular working day thus generating an overtime slip. He said I wasn't cleared to be interviewed by internal affairs on a day off. In truth, this was the day that internal affairs, my attorney, and I could all get together the same day. All other days we had conflicts. I was told that I had to be interviewed by a certain date and this was the only date that worked. Besides, I had sought out and received permission from my watch commander as required by LAPD policy. Nevertheless, a complaint for insubordination was added to my neglect of duty complaint (audit). Failing to check a couple boxes on an audit sheet was definitely not a terminating offense but insubordination was. That was their plan. To get me before a Board of Rights and terminate me.

I have to admit that the next move by the department was both devious and brilliant. They had been defeated numerous times in their efforts to terminate me in a plethora of ways. So a new tactic was in order. In May of 2008, I was contacted by Detective III Chris Casey and Sgt. II Cory Palka. They told me that an anonymous complaint had come to their attention in which I was the victim of work place retaliation. Say again? They told me that they were told that I, Barry Brooks, may be the victim of a LAPD hostile work environment. Where had they been the last thirteen years? They were from the newly created Workplace Discrimination Unit of Internal Affairs Group. I doubted their veracity but I had worked with Corey when he was a police officer and I remembered him as a decent guy. So I unloaded on them about everything I had been through, my strategies and affirmative defenses going forward against the department. After our initial interview, I didn't hear from them again. It wasn't until a few months later when interviewed by internal affairs regarding the insubordination complaint that I realized that everything I had told Casey and Palka had been turned over to the investigators handling my complaint. This, of course, is illegal and a violation of department policy. As a victim and someone who has reported misconduct, everything I told them was confidential. It is somewhat analogous to the attorney-client privilege. A few days later, my name was finally published on the LAPD promotion transfer list going from Pacific to Wilshire Division. I was so happy. Finally, after thirteen years of fighting, I was getting my promotion. It would only last a day. The promotion transfer comes out city-wide once a month and has the name of everyone who is getting promoted from detectives to sergeants and all the way up to deputy chief. Everyone in the department reads it. So the day the transfer came out, I got a dozen phone calls from some supporters who knew what I had gone through and my long fight. The transfer could have fifty employee names on it. The next day, to my shock and surprise (you would think I would no longer be surprised by now), a revised transfer came out and was distributed city-wide. It had one line on it: Barry Brooks form "officer" Pacific Division to "sergeant" Wilshire Division cancelled; remains police officer. How embarrassing this was for every employee in the department and many throughout the city, thousands, would see this. I was told by the union that never before had the department created a separate transfer the following day just to keep one person from promoting. Then again, I was used to being the first around LAPD. A few weeks later, my promotion for detective would also be put on hold albeit a little more latently.

In June of 2008, my attorney, Larry Hanna, stopped my interview by two internal affairs investigators because he saw that they were trying to get me to lie and admit to something I didn't do. Larry was a bulldog and someone not to be messed with. He smelled a red herring. He became so upset that he called the commanding officer of internal affairs and told him he was cancelling the interview and accused them of misconduct. Two days after the interview, Larry Hanna fired off a letter to the inspector general asking him to be present during my next interview by Internal Affairs. He wanted someone impartial at the interview because he knew they were out for blood. This request, of course, was refused. The next month I was rescheduled and interviewed on the insubordination complaint. To no one's surprise, despite the fact that I had the watch commander's permission to be interviewed on my day off and it had been agreed upon by internal affairs, the complaint was sustained. The department, seizing the opportunity, ordered me to a Board of Rights knowing that the Board had the power to terminate me and now have a charge (insubordination) in which they could justify terminating me they were good to go. My only hope was to make a deal with a new branch of LAPD called the Dispute Resolution and Settlement Office. On September 8, 2008, my commanding officer at Pacific came up with a new menial task for me to perform. Since transferring me back to Pacific Division in February of 2008 after the complaint was filed from the Office of Operations QAAC unit, he had done everything to annoy me and given me every demeaning task he could think of. This time he sent me downtown Los Angeles to supply division to pick up a load of paper for the copier and fax machines used by the division. These were very heavy boxes that would normally require two people to load. I had no help. They were simply left for me on the dock. I started loading the boxes of paper into the trunk of the police car and felt a rip in my abdomen. I went back to work and reported the injury which was thought at the time just to be an abdominal strain. The next morning, I woke up to go to work and was in the shower. As I started to soap up my body, I felt a giant lump just above my navel. It was the size of an egg and it was just under my skin. I knew I wasn't pregnant so this called for medical intervention. I went to Hoag Hospital emergency room and was diagnosed with a strangulated umbilical hernia. I was immediately scheduled for surgery at UCLA Hospital. I was lucky enough to get my thoracic surgeon, Dr. Maish, who had repaired my hiatal hernia to complete the surgery. The surgery went well except for the fact that I died. No really. I woke up in the recovery room with my surgeon and my wife looking over me very concerned. My chest and diaphragm felt like someone had jumped up and down on it while I was under anesthesia. Turns out that my heart stopped during surgery. They had to perform CPR on me. That's why my chest hurt so badly. Subsequent to the surgery, I was seen by a cardiologist from Cedar-Sanai Hospital who diagnosed me with arrhythmia, low injection-fraction ratio, and an enlarged heart. They kept me in the hospital for an extra day and I was sent home around September 11th. The following day I received a phone call from my commanding officer's adjutant. I was being relieved of duty pending my Board of Rights which was scheduled for the third week in December. Talk about adding insult to injury.

I knew that they were going to terminate me with prejudice at my upcoming Board of Rights. My only chance was to make a deal. I had my union defense representative John Mumma make contact with Chief Perez in an effort to make a deal. What made matters more difficult was that I had gotten severe infections in my surgical wound from UCLA and it caused me to go back to the hospital and rip all the stitches out and pack it with gauze. The doctor's solution was not to treat the infection and then sew it back up again but to simply leave it open so it would heal from the inside out. This process would end up taking six months to completely heal. Meanwhile with my Board of Rights approaching quickly, I met with my attorney and went over testimony. We knew that the department would try to bring in my three prior complaints that have all been sealed by legal settlement so they could point to a pattern of misconduct to justify them terminating me. Mumma kept working behind the scenes and about two weeks before my Board of Rights, we struck a deal. The deal was that the department would drop count one, the insubordination and only firing offense and I would plead guilty to making a mistake on an audit (negligence) and take a four-day suspension. They would then, in exchange, promote me to the rank of sergeant going back to April of 2008 and I would agree not to pursue the detective promotion. This agreement was all but done and we had verbal commitments from Chief Perez.

However, at that time, I had gone down to Fiscal Operations Division because I was off on workman's compensation even though I was relieved of duty after the fact. Under California Labor Code 4850, a police officer who gets injured in the line of duty (IOD) is entitled to a year of full compensation and is tax free. Also, the police officer who normally contributes to his or her own pension fund is not responsible for making that contribution while of IOD. In other words, the eight percent of my pay that I normally contribute out of my bi-weekly paycheck is not supposed to be taken out and given to the pension fund. The municipality or in this case the City of Los Angeles is supposed to make the contribution on behalf of the officer. A few years earlier when I was injured and kept out of work for approximately six months, I discovered this labor code which no one I spoke to at the union (league) or within the department knew about. I went to fiscal operations division and confronted them. They tried to play it off as a mistake at first but then when I threatened to get the city attorney involved in the matter, they cut me a check from the pension fund for contributions which they never should have taken out. I then wondered if they had done this to me before. So I went back to fiscal operations division with dates of all my IOD time over my twenty year career (going back to the 1980s) and sure enough, every single time I was hurt on the job and placed on workers compensation (IOD), they had stolen money from me and as a result, there was an over compensation to the police and fire pension funds.

I wanted to further test my hypothesis and see if there was further indicia of fraud going on here. I knew of a few LAPD officers that had been injured on duty (IOD) over the years so I contacted them and advised them of my findings. I asked them to go down to fiscal operations division with the dates of their injuries. I had one LAPD lieutenant, two detectives, and two officers all go down to fiscal operations division with the aforementioned information. Guess what? Every single one of them was owed pension contribution refunds. Some injuries went all the way back to the 1980s. After finding out the results of my investigation, I quickly came to the conclusion that if five out of five, six out of six if you count me, all had money illegally taken out of their paychecks then it stood to reason that this was prima facie evidence of massive fraud. I took this information to the Los Angeles Police Protective League. I told them that it was their duty, since all of these officers paid union dues to the league to represent their interest, to do something about it. I was told point blank by a Los Angeles Police Protective that they realized the seriousness of the fact that the City of Los Angeles may be guilty of millions of dollars of theft and fraud from sick and even dying police officers. They also told me that this was an election year and that their political action committee had spent or were going to spend, if I remember correctly, $252,000 on Carmen Trutanich for the office of Los Angeles City attorney. The money was going to be spent on positive radio spots citing the endorsements of the San Pedro defense attorney by Los Angeles County Sheriff Lee Baca and Dist. Atty. Steve Cooley and praising Trutanich as "law enforcement's choice." The point was made to me very poignantly that if the league filed a lawsuit against the city of Los Angeles to get back the money owed to these officers, then it would be Carmen Trutanich that would have to defend against the lawsuit. This would make them adversaries. I was told point blank, "Why should the league file a suit when we have him (Trutanich) in our pocket?" Carmen Trutanich made his election run based upon a law and order and get-tough-on criminals platform. To drive home the point, he talked frequently about a murder conviction he won as a young prosecutor against a South LA gang member who was sentenced to death for a 1982 killing. Trutanich, who served four years as city attorney, bragged of how he hadn't wavered in his face-off with Barry Williams, whom he called "one of the most notorious and violent gang leaders in Los Angeles." However, years later, a federal judge would throw out and overturn Trutanich's magnus opus conviction against Williams' murder conviction and death sentence, finding that Trutanich's conduct, along with other errors at trial, "significantly undermined the integrity" of the guilty verdict. I had gone to the

Los Angeles Police Protective League several weeks before my Board of Rights was to take place. However, I already had an agreed upon deal with Chief Perez as discussed (supra). So I wasn't worried about the impending board because it was supposed to be cancelled in light of the deal. However, at last minute and just several days after I brought this to the attention of the Los Angeles Protective League, all of a sudden the deal was pulled off the table with no reason given. Someone had talked.

I was assigned an attorney for my Board of Rights case from the Los Angeles Police Protective League—Jodi Gonda. She had a good reputation and was recommended by John Mumma who I had a tremendous respect for. Jodi was very fiery and we had several heated discussions when it came to the strategy regarding my board. The biggest issue was preventing the departments advocate (prosecutor) from introducing three old complaints which by way of court settlement were sealed and not to be used to show a pattern of misconduct which can take a small charge of misconduct and justify termination by showing a long-standing pattern of misconduct. The board was now only a few days away and I was still recovering from a serious surgery, heart attack, infection, and hospitalization. In fact, even though I was relieved of duty on September 12, 2008, my actual status was IOD because of the surgery a few days before I was relieved of duty which was declared to be industrial related and thus workers compensation under California Labor Code 4850. My defense representative, John Mumma, and I had made several attempts to have the board postponed due to my illness. I think they wouldn't do it because they thought I was in Tier IV of the pension plan which would leave me a few weeks short of my lifetime pension. Extremely devious. They did not know, as I found out later, that I was actually in Tier III, which vested me at ten years and not twenty. Nevertheless, under the California Code of Civil Procedure and more specifically under California Evidence Code 701; "A person is disqualified to be a witness if he or she is incapable of expressing himself or herself concerning the matter so as to be understood, either directly or through interpretation by one who can understand him." This applies to quasi-judicial proceedings including administrative proceedings such as a Board of Rights. At the time of my board, I was still recovering from the aforementioned serious and debilitating injuries and under the influence of heavy duty pain killers such as oxycodone and vicodone. I was definitely not competent to testify in my own defense. So the department violated the code of civil procedure and the evidence code but they didn't care. They wanted my scalp.

After the Board was sworn in, the advocate did what I knew he would do and that was read into the record my prior complaints—the ones he was not allowed by court settlement to use. I already had precedent on this issue in that the department ruled in my two administrative boards for my promotions to sergeant and detective that because of my settlement with the department they could not use these complaints during my administrative boards. I had already told my attorney to object strenuously to these complaints being entered into the record. I was shocked when she stood up and told the board members that we would not be challenging the issue of these complaints being entered into the record. I looked at her and asked her what she was doing. She said she didn't want to piss off the board members by objecting. I told her that they were going to terminate me no matter what she did and that we had to make objections for the record so I could file an appeal or writ of mandamus after they terminated me. She didn't believe me. She thought she had everything under control. The trial went on and even my supervisor took the stand and testified that what I did by marking a copy of a report that was shredded anyway after it was used for an audit was not misconduct. That should have ended the proceedings there as far as guilt was concerned. However, I still had the insubordination tacked on to deal with which is a firing offense. The Board of Rights concluded two days before Christmas. Deputy Chief Beck, the chairman of the committee that included Captain Hushammer, and a civilian attorney Mrs. Cho, found me not guilty of insubordination and guilty of compromising and audit. No one really knew what that meant. How do you compromise and audit when even the department admitted the mistaken marking I made on a copy of an audit did not change the results of the audit? The penalty phase had to wait until the Christmas break. So I spent Christmas wondering if I would have a job and a career come New Year's. I had been found not guilty of the harshest charge and guilty of such a minor offense that the department's own expert said it did not even violate department policy. I had hope.

A few days after Christmas, I sat in the judgment seat awaiting my fate. Deputy Chief Beck read the punishment. His rationale for the punishment he said was the fact that I was overeducated. He preceded the punishment by trying to rationalize it by saying that I was so intelligent, had seven college degrees and twenty years of experience in LAPD that I should have known that my mistake would compromise the audit process which prior testimony had admitted it did not. The recommendation of the Board of Rights was termination of employment. My attorney looked at me with a stunned look. I said to her, "I told you." The civilian, Mrs. Cho, an attorney, voted not to terminate me. I had to call my wife and give her the bad news. It wasn't quite over yet however as the Chief of Police had to sign off on the punishment and had the power to reduce it. At the time of my verdict, Deputy Chief Jim McDonald was sitting in as Chief of LAPD for Chief Bratton, who at the time was travelling the world and being knighted by in England. The usual stuff a Chief of Police does. My neighbors, who were also Christians like me, had a close relationship with Jim McDonald and told me he was a very good Christian man. I appealed to Chief McDonald through some surrogates. Also during my Board of Rights, one of my long-time supervisors and friends, Sergeant Lane Bragg, had been a character witness for me. He became so outraged that the Board had terminated me over something that wasn't even misconduct that he told the departments advocate that he wasn't going to see the chief over the matter and lodge a complaint. Sergeant Bragg made his way over to the Chief's office and was met by two lieutenants which were adjutants for the Chief. He was stopped from getting to the chief's office. One of the lieutenants said to him, "We know why you are here. The advocate called us. We want you to know that Brooks was terminated for other things that you don't know about—not for the charges at the Board of Rights." Interesting how the rank of lieutenant starts with the word "lie." Sergeant Bragg was stunned that the department and Chief would come right out and admit that I was being terminated from something totally different than what I was charged with. A few years later, I would confirm the real reason I was terminated. Sergeant Bragg notified me and I had him write up an affidavit which we later submitted during an appeal. Deputy Chief McDonald, the so called Christian upheld my termination I think was for political advantages. I was a target for all of LAPD management. I had exposed their duplicity, double standard, and moral bankruptcy. Anyone in LAPD management would certainly get a feather in their cap for terminating me. So then, it was no surprise when within a year of terminating me, Deputy Chief Beck was promoted to Chief of LAPD and Assistant Chief McDonald was appointed Chief of Long Beach Police Department.

Most of 2009 was spent pursuing justice. The Los Angeles Police Protective League paid for my writ of mandamus to try to overturn my termination. Writs of mandamus are very difficult to win. The burden is extremely difficult to prove. A plaintiff has to show that the LAPD displayed a "manifest abuse of discretion." You pretty much had to show that they simply totally denied the evidence and the verdict was not in line with the evidence. Much like the Tom Brady case that went from an administrative hearing (like mine) with the NFL to federal court on appeal, it is very difficult to prevail. Courts loathe at the opportunity to overturn administrative and labor law cases based on Memorandums of Understanding. The odds of winning a writ of mandamus are estimated to being about ten to one against the person appealing winning. Unfortunately for me, Diane Marchant was given the responsibility to complete and file my writ of mandamus. This is not because Diane is a bad lawyer. She is very good at filing writs. It just so happens that she had already given notice to the league that she was retiring and moving out of state. I could tell that she really didn't want the case because she didn't think she had time to adequately complete it. She was right. She finished and submitted the writ without even speaking to me. I couldn't even get Sergeant Braggs' affidavit that the department admitted lying about why they terminated me into the writ. I lost of course. I then hired Philip Kaplan to try to make something of an appeal out of this mess. He tried and did his best. In a motion for reconsideration, he even got the judge to admit that he thought I had enemies within LAPD management but it wasn't enough. In the end, I settled with the City of Los Angeles and received a paltry $25,000 in exchange for promising not to sue over my termination. At least I got something.

One lesson I had learned in my relationship with the Lord was that He means what He says and He says what He means. In April of 2008, I finally, after thirteen years of toiling against the LAPD machine, was going to be promoted to both sergeant and detective. It was at that time that the Lord told me that He was going to take me out of LAPD after twenty years of service had been completed. I fought Him. I said, "Lord, it was you that brought me three thousand miles to a foreign place where I knew no one. It was You that gave this career and told me you had a promise and a purpose for me. I am finally winning and getting my victory to be promoted after thirteen years of suffering and now you are going to take me out of LAPD?" I wouldn't have it. Of course the Lord knew that I was being idolatrous. I had fought so hard and for so long to get this promotion and recognition from my peers that it became idolatry. I put my promotion and reputation ahead of the Lord. So the Lord told me He was going to remove me from LAPD on my twentieth year. I was hired and my first day in the LAPD academy was September 12, 1988. I received notice of being relieved from duty and intent to terminate employment on September 12, 2008. Twenty years to the hour. The Lord means what He says.

A Future Promise from God

‹ ✦✦✦✦✦ ›

By May 2010, I had become depressed. Even though I technically didn't leave LAPD until March of 2009, I had been gone from it and off payroll since September 12, 2008. As discussed, the first couple of years after being terminated were really just shock. Just prior to being fired, I had finally one my greatest victory and court battle. I was going to make both sergeant and detective and in fact be the first person in the history of LAPD to be promoted to both on the same day (at least on paper). Besides, who gets fired for making a mistake on an audit? Although in hindsight, I should have seen it coming, knowing how desperate they were to find any excuse to get rid of me and being warned beforehand. Nevertheless, I acted not as a man of faith but as a man of the flesh. My immediate focus was not on God but how, right after my fourth child had been born, with my wife not working, could I keep my house, my lifestyle, my custom of living in Orange County? I had spent the first couple of years desperate to get back into law enforcement putting in applications everywhere but God closed every door and opportunity. I started to get mini seizures that we thought were linked to my cardiomyopathy. Very strange feeling of suddenly getting a cold chill and then oxygen deprivation followed by a sense that I was floating out of my body. My cardiologist called it a type of syncope. I would lick my lips and smack them together while rubbing the fingers on my left hand together while it went numb. My neurologist thinks it may be from some brain damage I suffered on the job when I was hit over the head with an aluminum pipe. I was leaking cranial fluid out of my nose for a few weeks and had very bad vertigo when it first happened. The prevailing thought from this doctor is that adhesions or scar tissues may have formed in my brain causing these seizures. Nevertheless, they were frightening and would come in waves for about two to three weeks at a time and then go away mysteriously for a month. I couldn't sleep at night and found myself on anti-anxiety medication or sometimes Ambien to get some sleep. I would only take these at night and I never abused them.

As has been His pattern in my life, God shows up at various times but usually when I need Him the most. One Sunday in May of 2010, I was getting ready to take my family to Calvary Chapel Costa Mesa for third service at 11:15 a.m. When I got up in the morning and started to wake everyone for breakfast, I soon realized that most of the household was sick. My wife was sick, my youngest, Elizabeth who was almost two years old was sick, my daughter Sarah who was three and one half was sick, and my son Mark who was nine years old was sick. The only one besides me that wasn't sick was my eldest child, Rachel who was eleven years old at the time. So when it came time to go to church just Rachel and I went. I dropped her off at Sunday school and happened to notice that her usual Sunday school teacher wasn't there. I didn't think much about it. I took my usual seat outside the main sanctuary where they have a large screen that carries the service live as well as audio. I didn't like going inside in sitting among the congregation. Crowded, noisy, and the worst part was the perfume and cologne. I am highly allergic to most perfumes and colognes and just about any scent that was manmade. I felt bad for my wife because she could never wear perfumes or use hair products that were perfumed or a lot of the girly stuff women wear. Calvary Chapel was a very large church. One of the largest churches in Southern California. This made it quite difficult getting in but especially out of the parking lot at the end of services. I would usually do one of two things. I would stay after service and take the kids to the small playground on campus since it was also a K-12 school there was a few playgrounds. I would let the kids play for about fifteen minutes until traffic in the parking lot started to thin out. I would then load them up and take them home or wherever else we needed to go. The other alternative was to sneak out early. As pastor Chuck or Brian was ending the service with a prayer, I would give my wife the nod and she would get a predetermined set of two of our children and I would get the other two and we would meet at the car just as the service was letting out and get out just ahead of the mass exodus.

On this occasion, I had the latter strategy planned. Since it was just me and my eldest daughter, who at eleven didn't have a whole lot of interest playing on the monkey bars, I was going to conduct a speedy extraction of her and hit the road fast. At least that was my plan. However, about fifteen minutes before the service ended I was approached by a guy who introduced himself as Gil. He said he was in charge of security at Calvary Chapel and wanted to talk to me. He told me that he has heard I was LAPD. I told that I was but I was terminated and was fighting it. He asked me to join the security ministry which was an all voluntary ministry of a mixture of guys with some background in security and a few with military or law enforcement backgrounds. We talked for a while and before I knew it the service was over. We talked for about another ten minutes and I told him that I really wasn't interested in joining his team until I either got back into another law enforcement agency or back with LAPD. One of the strangest feelings of being a cop all your life is suddenly not having the ability of having a gun with you everywhere you go. You feel naked. Every time I left my house, I would check the chamber of my weapon, check for extra magazines, etc. I had worked some very bad areas of Los Angeles and had put a lot of very violent killers, gang members, rapists, etc., in prison and had enemies. Having my weapon off-duty had just probably saved my life just a few years earlier when I had to pull it on two Santa Ana gangsters who, after getting offended at me beeping my horn at them after they cut me off, reached under their seat for a weapon (note to self: ease up on the horn).

After my conversation with Gil was over I started heading to my daughter's Sunday school class to pick her up. I was late. When I got there, all the kids had been picked up except for my daughter Rachel. I walked in the classroom and over to where my daughter was who was still sitting down and either drawing or working on a craft. I was watching her quietly work and I don't think she knew I was there yet. All of a sudden, I get a tap on my back. I didn't like it. As a police officer who has trained himself in survival tactics, I never allowed anyone to come up behind me. Even off duty when my wife and I are strolling down a sidewalk enjoying some window shopping (okay, she enjoys window shopping) and I feel someone coming up on me from behind, I kind politely take her arm and pull her aside pretending to point to something of interest until the person passes. So I feel the tap on my back and immediate turn around with probably a glare in my eye I saw a man in front of me. He immediately said to me before I could get a word out, "The Lord gave me a word of knowledge for you." This being the now the third time I had heard this phrase uttered to me and in each case had been proven true I just said, "Tell me." He looked right at me and said the following, "The Lord wants you to know that He has a plan and purpose for you in these end times. You are to step out in faith and get your house in order." The next Sunday while I was at Church and was pondering this word of knowledge and evaluating it as it applies to my life going forward, I ran into the wife of the man who had given me the word of knowledge the week before. She recognized me and as though she could read my thoughts she walked up to me and said, "Know that what my husband told you was from the Lord. That is his spiritual gift and if he told you it came from the Lord it did." She also told me that the Lord had given her a scripture to give to me to stand on until the Lord fulfills his promise to me. The biblical passage was Psalms 37:7-28. It was a Psalm written by King David and it states the following: "Be still before the LORD and wait patiently for him; do not fret when people succeed in their ways, when they carry out their wicked schemes. Refrain from anger and turn from wrath; do not fret—it leads only to evil. For those who are evil will be destroyed, but those who hope in the LORD will inherit the land. A little while, and the wicked will be no more; though you look for them, they will not be found. But the meek will inherit the land and enjoy peace and prosperity. The wicked plot against the righteous and gnash their teeth at them; but the Lord laughs at the wicked, for he knows their day is coming. The wicked draw the sword and bend the bow to bring down the poor and needy, to slay those whose ways are upright. But their swords will pierce their own hearts, and their bows will be broken. Better the little that the righteous have than the wealth of many wicked; for the power of the wicked will be broken, but the LORD upholds the righteous. The blameless spend their days under the LORD's care, and their inheritance will endure forever. In times of disaster they will not wither; in days of famine they will enjoy plenty. But the wicked will perish: Though the LORD's enemies are like the flowers of the field, they will be consumed, they will go up in smoke. The wicked borrow and do not repay, but the righteous give generously; those the LORD blesses will inherit the land, but those he curses will be destroyed. The LORD makes firm the steps of the one who delights in him; though he may stumble, he will not fall, for the LORD upholds him with his hand. I was young and now I am old, yet I have never seen the righteous forsaken or their children begging bread. They are always generous and lend freely; their children will be a blessing. Turn from evil and do good; then you will dwell in the land forever. For the LORD loves the just and will not forsake his faithful ones."

It was not the most direct word of knowledge I had ever gotten but this was the third time now the Lord had told me to get my house in order. I immediately thought of 1 Timothy 3:1-7 which states; "Here is a trustworthy saying: "Whoever aspires to be an overseer desires a noble task. Now the overseer is to be above reproach, faithful to his wife, temperate, self-controlled, respectable, hospitable, able to teach, not given to drunkenness, not violent but gentle, not quarrelsome, not a lover of money. He must manage his own family well and see that his children obey him, and he must do so in a manner worthy of full respect. (If anyone does not know how to manage his own family, how can he take care of God's church?) He must not be a recent convert, or he may become conceited and fall under the same judgment as the devil. He must also have a good reputation with outsiders, so that he will not fall into disgrace and into the devil's trap." At this point in my life, the stress of not getting back into law enforcement coupled with having been trapped in my house now for a couple of years with four winey, crying, and generally aggravating children had left me on my last nerve. Don't get me wrong, I love my children. They are a direct gift from God as my wife and I could not have children until God supernaturally intervened. Even though the noise they generated grinded on my last nerve all the time, I loved them and am thankful for them. I was also thankful that the Lord had looked ahead and knew what he was going to do in my life and provided a way to make a living by teaching college. I was thankful that the Lord had provided for me by pushing me to enroll as a college professor in community college back in 1996 when I earned my first master's degree. Little did I know at the time that He would eventually use my profession as a way to make financial ends meet while he was working out His plans in my life post LAPD. I earned another master's degree, then another and another and then a doctorate. I moved up from community college to four-year universities to teaching graduate school. Even though I was going off to work two nights a week to teach, the majority of my teaching was being done out of my home office teaching online. Even when I wasn't teaching out of my office, I was preparing lectures or grading about one hundred papers a week or posting lectures online. It was extremely difficult trying to grading graduate level thesis when your son who has set up his play station game with a 42" screen in the garage that shares a common exterior wall to my office. All I hear is the bang, bang, boom and audio of characters in the game screaming out orders and things at each other. It sounds like it is emanating from inside my office. I have a daughter that is in her room above me blaring out the Jonas Brothers and Demi Lovato and all those Disney artists coming through the ceiling at me. Then, add my four-year-old cranking Sponge Bob on the big screen in the living room next to my office and my two-year-old who keeps pounding on the locked office door wanting to sit in my lap. My wife thinks it's unreasonable for her to have to keep the house quiet for me. So I had become very moody. My kids were telling my wife after they tested my patients for the thirtieth time and I screamed at them that daddy's a monster today. I even started cursing at some points. It was becoming a little scary. Between the stress, lack of sleep, and the hangover from taking sleeping pills, I was a volcano half the time ready to erupt. My wife started calling me bipolar. Great mood one minute and then a monster the next minute. I didn't find out until a few years later that I was also slowly being poisoned by a medication I had been on since my surgery in 2008. It was slowly killing me, causing damage to my heart, liver, kidneys, bones and other side effects. More on that later. Nevertheless, I was becoming the one thing I never thought I would become—a hypocrite. I pray with my kids at night and take them to church on Sunday. I bought them Bibles and explain to them the importance of God being first in their life. Then they see and hear me scream and have a tantrum and it didn't take much. I hated the thought of my kids, especially my older ones, who hear me say one thing but then watch me do another. How can they ever really trust God with their lives and they see a father who claims to love the Lord and be Spirit-filled full of anger all the time?

So here was God calling me out again and telling me to get my house in order. I had an excuse however. Not a legitimate one but a rationalized one. I kept telling myself that as soon as I get back into law enforcement or win my case against LAPD or even find a good job that would get me out of the house (the cause of my stress I would say), then everything will get back in order. After all it was a catch 22. How could I get my house in order if the cause of me not getting it in order (being home) was contributing to it being out of order? I had it all figured out. Anyway, this part of God's word to me (getting my house in order) would prove to be the most elusive to overcome so I focused on the latter half of God's Word to me— stepping out in faith. I wasn't completely sure what God meant by stepping out in faith. However, I had a standing offer to join the security ministry just offered to me a few days earlier so I figured that would be part of my stepping out in faith. So I joined the ministry. I also started becoming more open and giving my testimony more at the university. I found that the more I stepped out on a limb by sharing my faith with my students, sometimes as a class, sometimes individually, the more God responded to my obedience and sent students to me. I believe that sharing one example with you of how God has used my position as a college professor to bring people to Him will illustrate my point. Remember, God is willing to use anyone for His purpose and glory so don't be surprised if you pray for this and He does exactly that.

I was teaching a class in Murrieta, California. I think it may have been criminology or perhaps research methods but it was an undergraduate class. This was a class of about fifteen students that was mixed gender-wise and ethnicity-wise. These classes were compressed five week courses that met once a week for four hours a night from 6 p.m. until 10 p.m. The first hour of the first week of each course, I introduced the syllabus and gave my grading polices. I also went around the room and had students introduce themselves. I then gave my introduction and I would usually throw a hook out there to the audience. I would mention that I volunteer in the ministry or talk about having earned a master's degree in theology or somehow get it out there that I was a Christian. During my introduction to the students, I would tell them how it was God that brought me from Massachusetts to California to join the LAPD. It was spiritual bait. So this class was going along well when we entered the fourth week of the class. After lecturing and giving an exam, I let the class out a few minutes early. There was one Hispanic girl in my class that was very quiet in the class. She didn't talk much or associate with the other students. After all the other students had left, she approached me at the podium and started a little chit chat about irrelevant things and then after she looked and saw no one was left in the classroom she asked me the million-dollar question—is God real? She started telling me how she was raised as a little girl in Mexico. In fact, she was raised as a Jehovah's Witness which astounded me. I thought all Mexicans were Roman Catholic never mind JWs. Being raised a Jehovah's Witness as a kid is horrible. Put aside the fact for a moment that it is a cult, they cannot celebrate anything. One of the more well-known practices of the Jehovah's Witnesses is their non-celebration of holidays. All holidays, including birthdays, are considered pagan holiday" and may not be observed by Jehovah's Witnesses. They say that Jesus never commanded Christians to celebrate his birth. Rather, he told his disciples to memorialize, or remember, his death. (Luke 22:19, 20) Christmas and its customs come from ancient false religions. The same is true of Easter customs, such as the use of eggs and rabbits. The early Christians did not celebrate Christmas or Easter, nor do true Christians today so they claim. The only two birthday celebrations spoken of in the Bible were held by persons who did not worship Jehovah. (Genesis 40:20-22; Mark 6:21, 22, 24-27) The early Christians did not celebrate birthdays. The custom of celebrating birthdays comes from ancient false religions. So imagine growing up as a kid and seeing all your friends get birthday presents and Christmas presents and Easter baskets and participate in other festivities but you couldn't. My next door neighbors growing up in rural Massachusetts were Jehovah's Witnesses. I saw it first-hand. So she continues to tell me how she was molested as a child and how she would pray to God and beg Him to stop the incest and molestation but it continued up into her teen years.

After about fifteen minutes of letting her get all those emotions out and crying and legitimately wanted to know if God was real and if He was, did He care about her suffering? Did He love her? Did He want a relationship with her? I looked at her and I said, "So your question is—how can I know if God is real?" She shook her head in acknowledgement, still weeping and choking back tears. I looked right at her and I said, "That's easy!" "I thought you had a hard question for me," I said. She looked at me incredulously as if she expected a five-minute exegesis and lecture on how each of us must find God on our own path. I said to her, "Here is your homework. Here is what you are going to do until I see you next week (the last week of class). Starting tonight, go home, find a quiet place in your home or apartment that is dark and free of noise. Get down on your knees to show respect and say the following prayer from the bottom of your heart. If you don't mean it, don't pray it. Say the following: "Lord God, if you are the God of the universe, if you are the God of the Bible, if you are the Father of Jesus and if He is your Son that you sent to die for my sins, please make yourself known to me." I told her that I wanted her to pray that prayer out of total sincerity, from the bottom of her heart every night until I see her the following week in class. She said "That's it?" I explained to her that God's word never returns void. That God in His word says, "Behold, I stand at the door knocking. If anyone hears my voice and opens the door, I will come in and eat with him, and he with me" (Revelations 3:20). I told her that God is standing there knocking on the door hoping that she will respond to His call. I told her that it is not His wish that anyone should perish that he wants all to come to Him—including her (John 3:16). I gave her my Jeremiah 29:11 speech and told her that God has an awesome plan and purpose for her.

She departed with her homework assignment I had given her. I sat there for a few moments and thought about what had just transpired. I had given my testimony many times to different students and people and used it to plant the seed in them that God loved them and had a plan and purpose for them but I had never been directly asked before if God was real and if so How does someone find out? I knew it was the Holy Spirit speaking through me and not my own words so I felt comfortable with what was said. Still, I had given her a guarantee that if she did what I told her to (through the Spirit) she would find out once and for all if God was real. That week went by slowly. I prayed every night for God to reveal Himself to her and to show Himself to her. I was full of both anticipation and a little trepidation. The following week, as class got started, she came in a little late after I had started my first lecture of the evening. I tried to catch her eye from time to time to try to get an indication one way or another if she had got her answer. Break time came and she darted off and didn't say anything to me. I began to have doubts. She again came in few minutes late from break as my second lecture started so I couldn't have a quick conversation with her. My curiously grew as the evenings class came to a close. At the end of class as most of the students were leaving, I finally caught her attention and I said to her with hands raised in the air and shoulders shrugged, "So?" I said. She looked at me and said, "Nothing happened." I looked at her and said kind of smugly because she didn't sound convincing, "Nothing? Are you sure?" She shook her head and walked out of the classroom. However, my spirit and my discernment said otherwise. Nonetheless, it was the last day of class and she wouldn't be back and I probably wouldn't have her again as a student so what could I do? The following day, I was checking my university emails when I saw in my inbox an email with this student's name on it. I opened it up and I read the first line which started out. "Dr. Brooks, I am sorry I lied to you yesterday about what happened to me when I was praying as you told me to." Before I started reading the rest, I noticed that her email was five pages long. I went back and started reading her email. She said that on her third or fourth night in prayer that God raptured her to what she thought was heaven and showed her her entire life starting when she was a little girl. She saw herself being molested and other things and God explained to her and showed her the bad things that happened during her youth and how they made her the way she is now (doubting God's love and plan). He told her that then as is now, He was always by her side. He never forsake her or left her. Then He told her His plan and purpose for her and many other things. I could tell that she was both very excited at times and at times she was weeping while she wrote this email. It reminded me of when God had raptured me to heaven several years earlier in my response to wanting to see His glory. She went on to try to describe some of the things she saw in heaven while there and many other things. I was amazed. If people only realized how eager God is to want to enter in and have a relationship with us they would seek Him diligently. We are His children, a royal priesthood. The best thing is that it is a free gift for the taking.

Saved from Afghanistan

In 2011, while still trying to figure out a way back into the LAPD, I had now been turned down by about twenty different police departments. It didn't make sense to me. Here I was with close to thirty years' experience in law enforcement; twenty with LAPD, and ten more combined with the military police, sheriff's department and US Marshals. I also had seven college degrees including five graduate degrees and had almost twenty years' experience as a college professor teaching criminal justice and law. Being home almost every day with four young children making lots of noise made it extremely difficult to grade papers and teach online. I started looking for any way out of the house since law enforcement was not working. I applied for a position as a law enforcement embedded personnel (LEP). This is where the Department of Defense or a designated contractor hired former police officers to go to Iraq or Afghanistan in this case to be embedded in a platoon of United States Marines. Police officers go out on patrol with Marines and teach them how to make arrests, interrogate, preserve evidence for prosecution, and basic police work. It did carry the risk of being blown up by an IED or shot in an ambush. It seems crazy that a father of four young children would risk his life like this but I was desperate. It wasn't so much financial desperation as times were hard but we were making ends meet. It was mental fatigue from being overexposed to my family and of course years of frustration from dealings with the LAPD. I wanted out of the house and I wanted action. If I had to risk my life or kill a few terrorists along the way, I was fine with it. I had two former partners of mine in LAPD who were in active reserves and called up to active service that were killed by IED in Afghanistan but it didn't matter because I had my mind made up. There was only one problem. I didn't fly. I had always had a fear of heights and in fact joined the SWAT team in the Army National Guard to help me get over that fear. They trained and repelled from a ten-story makeshift building. The same type that firefighters train on. Coming back from Europe in 1996 en route from London to Los Angeles over the Pacific Ocean, we ran into a lot of turbulence. I got tossed around the plane pretty good. However, the most difficult thing was when the plane would take a sudden dip kind of like the feeling you get on a roller coaster when you speed down a decline and your stomach feels like it's in your throat. Probably why I have never been on a roller coaster before. Panic set in and along with my fear of heights just changed something or heightened something in my subconscious. I only flew one more time after that event which was to attend my mother's funeral in 2001 in Massachusetts. It took a lot of Xanax and my wife's companionship to get me on that plane. I was shaking and pale the entire way. After I came back, I vowed never to fly again. Can you take a boat to Afghanistan?

By this time, I was being obedient to God in that He had called me to step out in faith and so I had joined the security ministry at Calvary Chapel Costa Mesa. One Sunday, about three weeks before I was due to go to Afghanistan, I ran into an LAPD officer named Brandon Vasquez. Brandon was young, had been assigned to LAPD's elite Metropolitan Division, and was a recent convert to Christianity. He told me that he had recently been placed on suspension from getting into a bar fight off-duty. This incident and being relieved of duty had driven him to the Lord. Due to the fact that he was in the Marine Reserves and no longer being paid by LAPD because of the indefinite suspension, the Marine Corps put him on active reserve duty as a favor to give him a paycheck. He was assigned to Camp Pendleton which was close by. He told me that they had an opening in something called the combat-hunter program. They were looking for someone who had been in the military, had a background in law enforcement, teaching and creating curriculum. I had all four so this was definitely my milieu. I met with his commanding officer and I was hired right away. It wasn't a bad job. It was only about a thirty-mile commute one way which was relatively short. It gave me the rank of a GS-13 which is equivalent to a major or lieutenant colonel and paid about $70,000 a year with lots of benefits. So for three months I would go off to Camp Pendleton (Camp Tallega) from 7 a.m. to 4 p.m., throw on a suit and tie and then drive to either Murrieta or San Diego to teach a four-hour class at the University of Phoenix and get home by midnight. Long day but it got me out of the house. I liked being back in the military with its top down chain of command structure much like law enforcement. The program was considered so important that Marines that were heading out to combat were mandated to take the combat hunter program. All was not well however on the domestic front. My father lived in a small town in Massachusetts in which I was raised called North Reading. Except for that drugged-out flight to bury my mom in 2001, I had not flown now in fifteen years. My father was afraid of flying and had never stepped on an airplane even though he served in the Navy at the end of World War II. So we lived three thousand miles apart and my father had lost most of his hearing by now. It was extremely difficult to speak on the phone with him. It was a lot of "What?" "Huh?" "What did you say?" So I started writing letters to him in which I felt more comfortable to let out some emoting. When I was thirty-five years old and had been in Los Angeles for ten years, I realized that I had never told my father that I loved him. He, as well, had never told me that he loved me. My father was very stoic and one of the greatest generations of Americans. He, much like his generation, didn't believe a man should show his emotions. Tough it out. Don't complain. In his mind, he showed love by providing for his family. So I made a determination that I was not going to die or more likely have him die without telling him that I loved him. I picked up the phone and dialed the number. After a few moments of pleasantries and inquiries of health, I was nervous and looking for an opening to tell him I loved him. Finally, at the end of our conversation when I was getting ready to say goodbye, I said kind of quietly but firmly, "I love you, Dad." Long silence, an awkward silence. Finally, after what seemed like an eternity, I heard a quiet but nevertheless sublime "I love you too."

By my third month teaching the combat hunter program, my dad was very ill. I was deathly afraid of getting a phone call from the 978 area code that would be a call from one of my brothers or sisters telling me my father had passed away. I had already experienced that with my mom ten years earlier but this time I know I wouldn't get on a plane. What would I do? The only other options were a three-to-four-day train ride or three-day automobile trip which would probably be too late and take a week round trip which I couldn't afford to miss that much work and still keep my job. Then God upped the anti. Someone with the Marine Corps made the brilliant observation that it would be cheaper to fly my team, consisting of about five non-commissioned officers and three of us subject matter expert instructors, around the world to different Marine bases that it was to fly all the Marines based around the world to Camp Pendleton to be taught by us. I came to work one day and got the news. "Guess what, Barry?" my commanding officer said to me, "We are now a travelling cadre instead of a stationary one. Next month we are flying to Hawaii for three weeks to train Marines." I looked at him and said deadpanned, "Hawaii huh? That's a long swim." "What do you mean?" he said. "Sir, I don't fly," I responded. He looked right at me as if finally realizing I wasn't kidding him and told me that I couldn't keep my job if I didn't fly. No pressure.

So I had three weeks to figure out how to get on a plane. This was compounded by the fact that my dad had recently been diagnosed with stomach cancer and had about a month to live. I immediately started fasting and praying. More praying than fasting as I have never been good at fasting being a body builder and power lifter. I had nightmares every night about crashing and dying in a plane. It wasn't so much the dying part that I worried about because I know where I am going when I die. It was the crashing part that scared me. My biggest fear is that the plane somehow gets disabled and goes into a death spiral. That long fall out of the sky being thrown around the airplane and having that sick feeling I get from being on a roller coaster was the issue. Everyone screaming we are going to die. I don't mind getting into a plane crash if it blows up at 40,000 feet and disintegrates. I am going to die immediately. I won't feel a thing. The nightmares got worse and I felt sick. I lost my appetite and didn't eat much as I was sick to my stomach. I spoke to my good friend and mentor Craig Hawkins. He had been one of my professors when I attended Trinity Law School. He was also a well-known apologist who had his own radio show and was a published author. I always went to him when I had an important decision to make for fellowship and advice. We talked, he gave me some books on getting over fear, and the fifty-thousand-foot view of the situation. Craig would say, "Barry, what's the big deal? So you die in a plane crash? You get to immediately go be with the Lord in heaven." Craig had a way with confronting things head on. No touchy feely approach with him which I did enjoy. The nightmares continued the following week with less than ten days before I was due to leave for Hawaii.

I came home that day and my wife put forward what seemed to be a crazy idea. She told me that she had been watching the television show *Real Housewives of Beverly Hills.* She had saw a hypnotist named Tom Silver who was a guest on the show and cured one of the housewives of her fear of flying in one session. It sounded crazy to me. I thought hypnotism was a bunch of mumbo jumbo. Still, I was desperate. I went down to Calvary Chapel Costa Mesa where I attended church and was a volunteer in the ministry to seek some sage advice. I broached the subject with a pastor and friend of mine and asked him if hypnotism was compatible with Christianity. The bible does forbid things like witchcraft and sorcery which comes under the same Greek word for drugs—pharmakeia (Galatians 5:19). According to the Greek dictionary defines it as: "witchcraft, magic, the use of spells and potions of magic, often involving drugs—a magic spell. It is a fact that witchcraft and magic in the Greek world often involved the use of drugs either by the witch or the one on whom the magic is worked.

However, my pastor opined that he thought that there was enough credible science behind the use of hypnotism to give it a try. So I conducted an internet search for hypnotist Tom Silver and cross-referenced it with the *Real Housewives of Beverly Hills.* I found out that he lived or at least had an office in West Lake Village, California which was a very upscale city in Ventura County about two hours' drive from my home in Orange County. I call him up and made an appointment. It should be pointed out that I had never heard of this man in my life or met him. I went to see him on Monday, five days before I was due to fly to Hawaii or Boston should my father die first. Six-hour flight either way. When I first met Tom, he seemed like a nice enough guy and we talked a little before we conducted the session. He told me that all of his hypnotherapy sessions were recorded and that he would provide me with a compact disc of the session after each session to keep. This was a safeguard I believe against any allegations of illicit behavior during the session. I was a little dismayed that he volunteered to me that his life had been in turmoil and that he was now starting out on his third marriage and had problems with alcohol. I guess I thought it would take someone who had their act cleaned up to fix someone else's problems. Nevertheless, I went through with the session and don't remember a whole lot. I do remember walking out of there saying to myself that this guy was messed up. How is he going to help me if he can't help his own life? None of the fear of flying was alleviated when I left his office that day. I was very discouraged. The next day, the Lord heavily impressed upon me that I needed to go back to see Tom again before I flew to Hawaii. That is, if I would even go to Hawaii because at this point, the nightmares, queasiness, lack of sleep, and loss of appetite had me starting to lean in the direction of quitting my job rather than getting on that plane.

I decided to heed to the Lord and made an appointment to go see Tom on Thursday, two days before my trip to Hawaii was due to depart with my job on the line. I sat in the chair I had just sat in a few days before and as Tom counted me down for the hypnotic session, 5, 4, 3, 2, 1. He said something to me that got my attention. He said, "Barry, as you go into this session and relax, I want you to think about two things; your family and your faith." This really got my attention because I had not told Tom I was a born again Christian. I had not mentioned anything about my personal faith or convictions. I could have been a Buddhist for all he knew. Still, throughout the session, I held on to that verbiage. As he counted me back out of the session, "You are feeling more and more awake and at the count of one you will be totally awake and refreshed, 5,4,3,2,1 and awake." I lifted my head and looked him straight in the eye and said to him, "You're a Christian aren't you!" Tom's eyes became wide and I saw a look of both surprise and bewilderment on his face. He said to me, "How did you know?" I told him that I knew God had sent me back to him for a reason. I said to Tom, "What's your story?" He told me that only a few years back he had destroyed his second marriage and was an alcoholic. He was contemplating suicide and one night found himself with a bottle of booze in one hand and a loaded gun the other. He was going to end his life. He made one last ditch effort to save his soul and cried out to Jesus for mercy. Tom stopped and looked at me and deadpanned, "and I am Jewish!" He told me that at that moment when he cried out to Jesus, he heard God speak to him and tell him, "This too shall pass." After that, he felt a total sense of peace and he dedicated his life to helping people, especially fellow Christians, with his gift. I walked out of his office that day walking ten feet tall and just amazed again at how God had arranged the circumstances so that Tom and I would cross paths. Oh yeah, my fear of flying was gone.

I flew to Hawaii with a fellow instructor and former National City Police Lieutenant named Lanny Roarke. I had a lot of fun and got a chance to minister to a few Marines with the gospel. I was gone for three days and returned home to Orange County on a Friday. The following day, Saturday, my father passed away. Free from the burden of missing my father's funeral, I booked a flight for my wife and I to head out to Boston. I had been praying for several decades now for my father to come to a relationship with the Lord Jesus Christ. He was a tough sell. He blamed God for taking his wife (my mom) too soon. I retorted to him that God had given him fifty years of marriage to the most wonderful woman in the entire world. God had given him five healthy children, eleven grandchildren, and five great grandchildren. My father was hospitalized the last few weeks of his life and I was three thousand miles away and unable to communicate with him. I was wrestling earnestly in prayer for him. After talking with my sister Julie at the funeral, it became clear that the Lord had sent someone who worked at the hospital to minister to my father and he accepted the gospel only a few days before his death. God is good.

On the flight to Boston to my dad's funeral, I was having a tremendous spiritual battle. I really wanted to use the funeral not only to bless my father but to bless God as well. During the flight and the two days leading up to the funeral, I felt like I had the proverbial devil on one shoulder and angel on the other. The devil would tell me not to preach Christ that there would be people at the funeral who would think I was a Christian nut job and that it would look like I was using the funeral and the opportunity in front of a microphone and audience to preach to a captured audience. The angel was telling me that there was someone at the funeral that needed to her from the Lord. There was one or more persons who needed to hear the Word of the Lord. I began to think of what my brothers and sisters would think. They always thought of me as a little odd in my dedication to the Lord. People who have an intimate experience with the Lord and a close relationship with Him see almost paranormal even to other Christians. It can come across as a holier-than-thou attitude. It can also just be interpreted, especially without proper context, as pure crazy and sanctimonious. I made a decision to speak from the Book of James after contemplating my father's life and his character. He was one of those strong silent types who acted out of love but never uttered the word love. So I decided that my dad was a doe" of the Word but not so much a sayer of the Word. After preaching Christ during the funeral and breaking down pretty miserably after trying to keep my composure, I was satisfied with what the Holly Spirit had put on my heart and my lips. I was not the only one. Several people came up to me after the funeral and thanked me for preaching the Gospel during the eulogy of my father. One of life's most difficult times was completed by honoring and being obedient to God.

The Penultimate Battle

You think that it would be enough that the LAPD spent thirteen years destroying my career, causing my health to falter, ultimately my temporary death but thank goodness that God had other plans. I was terminated from LAPD right around Christmas of 2008 and left the Department for good in March of 2009 when my surgeon finally cleared me to return to work. LAPD has five different pension plans depending on when you joined the police department. I was in Tier 3 which meant I was vested at ten years but could not collect until I was fifty years of age. I was forty-five years of age in 2008 when the fired me so I had to wait five years until I turned fifty to collect. It was a struggle dealing with all of the financial and emotional fallout of losing my career and being branded as untrustworthy. Trying to keep a family of six financially afloat when my wife doesn't work on a part-time college professor's salary was not easy. However, God always provided just at the right time.

On February 5, 2013, two things happened. First, I was now in my eighteenth year in battling LAPD and the City of Los Angeles which was still going strong. I also turned fifty years old and became eligible to collect my service pension for life. It wouldn't be a lot, about $35,000 a year which is a paltry sum compared to many of my contemporaries and former partners that have left LAPD for the lush pastures of Orange County who were making $100,000 a year or more for life. Nevertheless, it was something I earned that could help and would eventually be a nice supplemental income when the Lord places me wherever He puts me for my next career. In January of 2013, I went down to the City of Los Angeles Fire and Police Pension Retirement and put in my papers and notice to collect my pension when I turned fifty years of age in a few weeks. Everything went well at first, I met with a very nice counselor and sat down and did all of the calculations and beneficiaries as well as applicable policies and tax laws. Then came the phone call.

About two weeks after my completing the paper work, I was home with my wife and I received a phone call from a mid-level manager. She explained to me that when I left the police department four years prior (when I was terminated), I was supposed to fill out some paper work for my deferred pension. She indicated that she had no record of the aforementioned paper work and therefore I was going to be denied my lifetime service pension. It took a moment for those words to penetrate my skull. My wife was looking at me from across the room, listening in on the conversation. She told me that she saw my jaw drop and my face go ashen and then beet red. I stammered for a moment, mumbling something incoherently and then I covered the phone with my hand and silently mouthed to my wife, "They're denying me my pension." When reality sunk in, my law school education kicked in and I began a series of expositive questions: "What paper work?" "What is it called?" "How do I know you didn't lose it?" and so on. I have to admit that in a story line of incredible retribution, abuse of power, and retaliation that had gone back now eighteen years, I immediately felt mad at God. I started asking within myself to God; how could you let this happen? "Why would You let me get this far and deny me." Then of course the Lord quickly reminded me of all the things he has done for me when I have trusted Him. One of my favorite pastors, Charles Stanley, has a maxim he always lives by that I have adopted over the years; "Obey God and leave all the consequences to Him." I, of all people, should never be emotionally driven by my enemies here on earth. Certainly not after the legacy God had done in my life—and He wasn't finished.

So, another battle begins. The penultimate battle as it would turn out. I noticed that during my interviews with several different administrators and clerks from the Los Angeles retirement pension system that one woman seemed to be very sympathetic and empathetic toward my plight. I knew that if I was going to win this war which, like every other battle in this eighteen-year war, would be protracted, I would need a spy. Someone to gather me intelligence from within the system. One day I looked up this woman's phone number in the City of Los Angeles directory and gave her a call. She remembered me and said that she didn't think that what they were doing to me was right. The following week, we agreed to meet. She told me that in 2011, the City of Los Angeles Police and Fire

Retirement Office had sent out approximately two hundred forms to retired police officers to fill out and send back to the city giving notice of their intention to collect my pension (as if someone would not want their pension). All of the returned forms were lost by this one clerk. Mine was in that bunch. Instead of doing the right thing and resending out forms and make calls to notify, the mistake went uncorrected. I don't know how many other police officers who they may have denied their service pensions to but I can't imagine I was the only one. Then again it wouldn't be the first time they had used selective persecution against me.

Armed with this inside information, I wrote a letter to the head of the Retirement System relaying the facts. It was denied. I then contacted my informant who had been well entrenched in city government for a long time and knows how to get things done in a bureaucratic environment that is the City of Los Angeles. She told me that each department within the City of Los Angeles whether police, fire, work comp, Fiscal Operations, pensions, etc., all answered to a corresponding section of the Los Angeles City Attorney's Office. Under the Los Angeles City Charter and Administrative Codes, the city attorney has power to make decisions whether administrative or not, and order departments within the city to grant or deny petitions and appeals. I found out who is the head of the Retirement Board and wrote a letter using their own codes and explained in detail how it was through his department's negligence that I was being denied my pension and how given the past eighteen years of retaliation and harassment by the LAPD and City of Los Angeles that this was just a continuation of this pattern and practice. A few months went by and it was now May and no pension. I felt the need to go to prayer and meditation. I don't mean that I haven't prayed about it. I had been praying since February about the matter. For whatever reason, my wife and I had never prayed much together. Her having the prototypical Roman Catholic faith, was confirmed at fourteen and her ticket to heaven punched and then kind of left to eke out an existence without any real relationship with the Lord. My wife is awesome but like most other Roman Catholics I have met, had never been taught to have a relationship with the Lord at a personal level. It was all about giving loyalty to the Pope and the Roman Catholic Church. I, on the other hand, was continually thirsty to know God and had several what I will describe as Pauline like encounters with God. Once in a while, my wife and I would kneel at the foot of out bed and prayer about a situation. I don't know what it is about marriage but God seems to honor it. I know it is one of the three institutions He created to help us including government and the church. The Bible also states that "wherever two or more are gathered, there I will be in the midst" (Matthew 18:20).

So we prayed about the pension issue together with tears (mostly me), imploring God to give us this victory for the sake of our family and children and remind Him that he promises to take care of all our needs. In the middle of our prayer, the phone rang. It was a young lady from the pension department. She told me that they had decided to graciously give me my lifetime pension. I started to weep and my wife knew without even having to ask me the outcome. I hung up the phone and dropped to my knees and just wept. I turned to my wife and I said, "See, God is always faithful." I was so happy that the next day I called my informant to let her know what had happened. She said, "I know, they walked it over to the City Attorney's Office and they chastised them for being incompetent and ordered them to give you your pension." Of course the person that I had been dealing with, Robyn Wilder, and her bosses were upset and embarrassed. She played it off by telling me it was her autonomous decision to give me my pension. However, behind closed doors she smelled a rat and started looking for an informant. "There is no way he could know all those things that happened in this department without someone from the inside telling him," she said. I was happy. Another victory for me but the credit belongs to God.

During my career with LAPD and especially the eighteen years of retribution and retaliation I went through, one of the mechanism that helped me survive numerous attempts at trying to terminate me or discipline me or demote me was using the LAPD's own rules against them. I had learned more about how the LAPD operated and the City of Los Angeles since being terminated than my entire twenty-year career. I learned little nuances and how things were coded in the payroll and retirement system that meant a world of difference as to benefits and how you were perceived from the city. I learned how behind every city department whether payroll, retirement, human resources, risk management, etc., was a deputy city attorney in charge. For example, when the pension department tried to deny me my pension and I presented them with evidence to the contrary of their decision making, they would run to their immediate department head boss at the City of Los Angeles City Attorney's Office. It was a smart move. I had become very good at setting traps for the bureaucrats within the City of Los Angeles management. I sometimes would send an email to the department head with certain innuendos contained within the body of the message which I know would get a reaction out of them. I had one of my informants watch for a reaction. One time I sent an email to a very high ranking official in the pension department. You have to understand the way city government works. Often times, the city will come out and say that something you are asking is impossible because it violates policy or procedure or law. For example, earlier I discussed how the City Attorney's Office, after consultation with LAPD executives, told me that my request to seal or expunge complaints that I deemed false from my personnel record was impossible because it violated citizen's rights to have faith in a clear and transparent department in whose officers packages represented their employment accurately. They also told me it was a violation of the California Penal Code, Evidence Code, and City of Los Angeles Administrative Code. However, when I offered to take $100,000 less in my settlement, all of a sudden it became very doable.

So by setting up some informants in the pension and retirement system of Los Angeles, I was able to get inside information on deals that were cut behind closed doors. Because I joined LAPD in 1988, I was put in Tier III. LAPD has five different pension systems depending on when you came on the job. Those of us in Tier III were stuck at 2% per year at age fifty for retirement. Tier IV which came later, allowed for 2.5% with no minimum age (50) of retirement. Once you reach twenty years on, you became vested and could retire as young as forty-one years of age and for ten percent more than Tier

III police officers. The only catch was that in Tier III you vested at ten years, not twenty. So if you had eleven years on and resigned or were terminated, you could still receive a small but nonetheless lifetime pension. Officers like me who were in Tier III had an opportunity during our career to switch over to Tier IV. Many did. That ten percent extra proved very hard to resist for many officers. However, for that ten percent, they were giving up the security of being vested at ten years. This is why I believe the LAPD pushed so hard to accelerate my Board of Rights. I was within a couple of months of reaching my twenty-year in service vestment. What they didn't realize was that I was one of the few officers that didn't switch over to Tier IV. For some reason, they thought I was in Tier IV so they could get at me another way by terminating me a couple of months short of my twenty-year anniversary and vesting date. This is probably why they denied my attorneys motion to delay my Board of Rights because I was still recovering from major surgery. They didn't know I was already vested. However, for some reason they didn't know I was in Tier III. This is why even though I was in the hospital recovering from post-surgical severe stomach wound and infection and a heart attack while I was under anesthesia, they went ahead and held my Board of Rights anyway. I and my representative had asked for a postponement which they are supposed to grant under California administrative law and evidence code. You have to be competent to testify, defend and otherwise confront your accuser. I was in so much pain and on a cocktail of antibiotics, painkillers, and other medications that I was hardly coherent. Res ipsa loquitur!

The devil is in the details as they say and so it was with those officers that decided to switch over to City of Los Angeles Tier IV. Not only did the officer's pension vest now at twenty years instead of ten, but they couldn't get back their contributions either. Modernly, a lot of municipalities are struggling with public pension funding and investment. Often time's large chunks of the revenue go towards paying police and firefighters pensions. A new trend is emerging in which cities and counties are requiring police officers to make 100 % of their pension contribution. The city or county does not make or match it. When I was an officer with LAPD, we were one of the few police departments in which police officers pay their own pension contribution 100 %. For example, when I retired from LAPD after just about twenty years, my total contribution towards my pension was approximately $126,000. I was given a choice. Take the money and run with no pension or leave the money in and start collecting a lifetime pension when I vested at age fifty. It would be foolish to take the money out knowing that you will make it back in the first three years or so of your retirement. Well the other catch for those who switched over to Tier IV and put eight percent of their gross pay into the pension system was that if they resigned or got terminated a day before their twentieth anniversary hire date they lost it all. Not only did they not vest and qualify for a pension but to add insult to injury, the City of Los Angeles stole their money. Yes, I said stole. I don't know what else you would call it. An officer puts his or her life on the line over and over again and pays his or her own money into what is essentially a savings account controlled by the City of Los Angeles. An officer gets terminated with nineteen years and eleven months on the job, often for retaliatory or arcane purposes, and loses everything. No pension, none of their contributions back, no more career. I personally know of more than one officer that has committed suicide in such a case. In the real world, if I had money market account or a CD with a bank or even an IRA in which I made regular contributions to then I would be entitled to a return. It matures in twenty years. I may run into a hardship in life and have to pull my money out a little early. What is the most that would happen? Perhaps an early withdrawal and tax penalty but you would get your money back. I still call what LAPD does thievery.

Going back to my point of using the City of Los Angeles own policy and procedure against, it is here that I want to make my point. There was a time of open enrollment when those LAPD officers that were in Tier III were allowed to transfer over to Tier IV. It was kept open for a year and then closed never to be open again. However, like I said, there are always back door deals going on behind the scenes that do not get publicized. I wanted to test the veracity of a particular city department head. I sent a formalized letter under penalty of perjury to this particular department head and I indicated my request to transfer from Tier III to Tier IV. The immediate response back to me in writing was that once the door closed which I believe it had back around the mid-1990s, I wasn't allowed by policy to apply and receive a transfer to Tier IV. This was absolute. I was given a copy of the administrative order that came out back then and a copy of the City Charter and the Administrative Code and so on. They all forbid anyone from transferring pensions once the open enrollment had expired and definitely once a police officer had left the department in which case for me was 2009.

So there it was in black and white. I had one of the top administrators in the city send me a certified letter backed by laws, policy and codes denying me the ability to transfer from Tier III to Tier IV. I then contacted my informant who had access to meetings that were held off the record or not published. You see the city is not afraid of violating its own rules, policies, and even the law, as I demonstrated earlier with my settlement. What they are afraid of, very afraid of, is setting a precedent. If word got out that the city had allowed even one former police officer to transfer pension tiers, the flood gates would open. Often non-disclosure agreements (NDA's) were part of these types of settlements do they could not be used as test cases or as precedent. Remember that although a fair amount of police officers transferred from pension Tier III to IV, there were hundreds and perhaps even thousands that did not out of fear of getting terminated with nineteen years on the job and getting nothing. The chance to complete twenty years and not having that albatross hanging around your neck was a huge relief. To be able to then transfer to Tier IV and retire at twenty years at 50% instead of 40% and perhaps as early as forty-one instead of a minimum of fifty years was huge.

I was told by my informant that there had indeed been several cases in which the City of Los Angeles Retirement Pension Board had granted the transfer of several former LAPD officers from pension tier to pension tier. She gave me the name of the officers and the case and file numbers and even the members of the Board that were sitting that day. In fact, this manager was present at these meetings and gave her input to the Board prior to the decision being made.

These deals were kept off the record. I really wanted to make an example out of her and all the corruption, nepotism, and cronyism that went on there. So I decided to go one step further. I played dumb and I sent her a second follow up request for information. I said that I had received her denial and quoted all the reasons she gave me for the denial of my request. At the end of the letter I stated. "Please give me the name and case numbers of any employees that the board or that your department unilaterally or in conjunction with the Board granted tier transfer requests that you have cognitive knowledge of or should have or that any of your staff and/or employees would have knowledge of." Again, I knew what the response would be but I was painting her into a corner. A few weeks go by and I got a written response that denied any knowledge on all counts of anyone who had been granted a tier transfer outside of the open enrollment. Now I had her. I then crafted a letter which I CC'd (carbon copied) to the City Attorney's Office, her boss and her boss' boss. In the letter, I asked for a detailed explanation of why she and the board granted tier transfers to three different police officers that transferred not only after the open enrollment period had ended but years after they separated from the department. I gave the name of the officers, case numbers, dates and the fact that she was present when they occurred. I pointed out that she had lied to me and the fact that she misrepresented her department's position. Further, I cited federal statutes, state law on retaliation and disparate treatment of those similarly situated like me as was the other officers. I used key words that I knew as a department manager she would understand to carry overtones of criminal and civil liability.

Of course she was extremely shocked when she got my letter. Seeing that a copy also went to her boss and the City Attorney's Office, she was livid. Besides her hatred for me and the fact that she had been exposed in an outright lie, the biggest shock to her was exactly what I wanted her to know—that I had someone on the inside. She immediately knew that I had to have had help from someone on the inside of the organization and someone with intimate knowledge of how their system works. She sent out a department-wide notice in which a copy was forwarded to me by my informant. It was pretty pathetic. It was a warning and an order that said no one was allowed to help Barry Brooks. That was very brazen. Does she realize how damaging this email would be if it was introduced as evidence of retaliation, discrimination, or even a 42 USC 1983 case? It is part and parcel of the mentality of the LAPD and City of Los Angeles policy makers. They think they are untouchable. And they are! I have seen time and time again in which LAPD command staff officers get caught lying, losing evidence, and committing perjury and the department just rewards them by promoting them as long as they hold to the company line. This would never happen in the private sector. Some CEO causing the company to lose millions in lawsuits again and again is chastised by the courts as untrustworthy; displays incompetence in leadership time and time again, yet keeps moving up. I decided that this was a battle for later on and I had bigger fish to fry. However, just to keep them on their collective toes, I sent them a letter telling them that sometime in the near future, I was going to show up ex parte before the Retirement Board and demand on the record that I be transferred from Tier III to Tier IV and that I would read into the record all of the officers that they had made exceptions for in the past.

One of the biggest issues with me and with I think with most police officers especially big city police officers who face a lot of danger and become part of the brotherhood of the thin blue line is being on the outside. Your badge, your authority the ability to carry your gun on and off-duty becomes a part of who you are. There are very few vocations that you can't leave behind when you punch out. Police work is an unusual job because they things you learn and the instincts you develop stay with you. It kind of reminds me of that scene from the movie *The Bourne Identity*. Jason Bourne is in a restaurant trying to figure out who he is and he realizes that as soon as he walked into the restaurant he knew were all the exits were, who in the restaurant might pose a danger to him, the license plates of the cars outside, etc. Here I am as I write this book five years out of LAPD and I still go to restaurants and as soon as I walk in, I do a cursory glance around the room for people who might be dangerous, people I may have arrested, or came across in the past. I size up and profile everyone. I know where all the exits are. I usually try to get a table facing towards the main door so I can see everyone who comes and goes from the restaurant. Working in one of the most violent cities in America during one of the most violent times in urban American history causes you to create survival techniques and mechanisms that stay with you for life. I have been involved in a number of off-duty situations in which my training has caused me to see trouble coming. I can tell you right now that it has prevented me from being robbed at least twice, the victim of a carjacking, a road rage incident that was about to turn into a shooting and many other times when my instincts warned me of an impending incident and the fact that I was armed insured my survival.

When you get suddenly terminated from a position as a law enforcement officer, your entire persona changes. Your former friends that treated you as part of a special group of individuals now feel awkward around you. Your police identification that you carried around with your badge made you feel special. I will admit that coming home late at night at two or three o'clock in the morning from Los Angeles to Orange County I might have sped a little. A few times the California Highway Patrol pulled me over for going 80/65. Because I always had a gun in my middle console along with my wallet and police identification, I was always cautious when getting pulled over at night. I would pull over, turn my interior lights on, roll all my windows down, shut the car off and put my hands in plain sight usually on the steering wheel. As soon as they made contact, I would tell the officer who had already asked for my license, registration and insurance, that I was an off-duty officer and my driver's license, identification and weapon were in the middle console and then I would tell him, "What do you want me to do."

I wanted him to feel in control and know the situation so I don't get shot reaching in for my wallet and he sees my Glock. Even when I was terminated from the LAPD and lost my badge and identification for a period of time, my license plates on my car were still registered as confidential. I always made sure that my driver's license and license plates were confidential when run in the Department of Motor Vehicles database. Gangsters and bad guys often have intelligence as well and there were some instances in the past in which they would have a relative or girlfriend that worked at the Department of Motor Vehicles (DMV) and would get our home addresses. Once the driver's license and plates are in the DMV database as confidential, when they are run through the system it just pops up "Barry Brooks LAPD." There is no address or even personal descriptors available. Most police officers will run a license plate before they pull you over for safety purposes. If I am about to pull a car over with, for example, two male Hispanics in it, I want to know if the car is reported stolen or on a BOLA list (Be On the Look Out) before I make contact. So without my badge and gun, I did worry about getting accidently shot by a police officer on a traffic stop.

Then there is all of the civil service discounts and perks of being a police officer. Now I am not making an ethical judgment on gratuities. However, there are many perks, depending on department policy which vary, of being a police officer. I got into movies for free, restaurants, got into restricted areas of airports, courthouses, government buildings. Many of the big amusement parks in Southern California give what they call civil service discounts for police and fire. Modernly, they tend to give more discounts to the military and deservedly so. So there are more benefits to being a cop then just getting out of tickets. However, the biggest difficulty of losing the ability to carry your badge and gun is a sudden loss of identity. So to me, one of the biggest things I wanted besides my job back with the LAPD was to clear my name and get my badge and police identification back and all the privileges that came with it. God knew this was in my heart and once again, He orchestrated another miracle for it to happen.

I believe that God had put this informant, who I call my angel, in my life to help me. I believe that God puts people in our paths for reasons and seasons. So my angel that had risked her career to help me when the "dragon lady" was trying to stop me from getting my pension told me about a little known section in the California Penal Code. Once I reached retirement age (50) under pension Tier III, which I did in 2013, I was allowed to petition for a hearing to be granted my Carry Conceal Weapon permit (CCW) sponsored by the LAPD. This would be a three-member panel. One member would be from the Los Angeles Police Protective League (LAPPL) which was my union. The second member was chosen from within LAPD personnel, someone of management level status but civilian not sworn. Someone just like the dragon lady. The third member was supposed to be neutral and was usually an attorney picked from a list of city arbitrators or mediators. Once I turned fifty and became pension vested and once I successfully beat back the City's attempt at denying me my pension, I went down to the sergeant in charge of the retirement section that was responsible for scheduling and putting on these hearings. These hearings were only held twice a year—in July and in December. So by April of 2013, I had begun the push to get this panel convened so that I could attempt to win and get my badge and identification and ability to carry my gun not just in California but under HR 218 or the Law Enforcement Act of 2004, all fifty states. They call them fifty state badges.

The sergeant in charge of these hearings as it turns out was an old partner of mine. We had worked together at Pacific Division and he seemed like a really good guy. I am not sure if he is a believer or not but he treated me fairly. I was both excited and scared as it became May and I knew I was only two months away from something I dearly wanted. So I did what I usually do and that was to go to work preparing my case. Since I graduated law school and had learned a lot about how city government worked and the inner workings of LAPD and the City of Los Angeles, I had been pretty successful at filing my own lawsuits, writs, appeals, and administrative appeals and grievances. Right there was the problem. I was taking too much credit for my brilliant legal and writing skills and not giving enough (if not all) the glory to God. So God had to teach me again how to trust Him. I pushed hard to get that July hearing. I called Sergeant Mendoza a couple times a week. I called his assistance. I left messages and I even drove down town and dropped by a couple of times. I prayed a lot. I prayed to God that He would help end at least this part of my suffering by granting me the July hearing and a victory. At the beginning of July, I received a phone call from Sergeant Mendoza who told me that my hearing was going to be bumped back until

December of 2013. I was devastated. Another high followed by another low. I was disappointed in God and I told Him so. I, from my humanistic point of view, couldn't see the logic of delaying this hearing. If God can do all things and He can, why delay granting my petition?

It's not fair to God that we consistently and quickly forget how good He is to us. According to Jeremiah 29:11, He has a plan for every single person. One of the most tragic things for Christians is becoming born again (so heaven is assured) but then live our own life and make our own decisions without letting God guide us. Where God Guides, God provides. I think some Christians are afraid to seek God's will for their life because they think that God will make them a missionary and send them off to some remote tribe in the sub-Sahara. Another thing Christians very often forget is that God's timing is not our timing. As God says, "For my thoughts are not your thoughts, neither are your ways my ways," declares the Lord" (Isaiah 55:8-9). So once again, God would put me to this axiom to the test in my life. Soon it was August, then September, and then October. I was still battling the City of Los Angeles for the eight hundred hours of sick time they owed me since 2009 and about six months of Injured on Duty Time (Workers Comp) they owed me. I had submitted my two-hundred-page declaration hoping to get my Board of Rights reviewed as per the Chief' Beck's promise. I had a few discussions with Sergeant Mendoza during those months and he even hinted at my hearing being pushed back all the way to July of 2014 all though he wouldn't commit. So it did come to me as a surprise when he left a message on my home answering machine on November 18th that I was scheduled for my CCW hearing on December 3rd, 2013. I got an email the same day and an official letter the next day confirming the date. I went into full panic mode. I had only two weeks to prepare for the most important hearing of my LAPD career. Getting my badge, identification, gun and reputation back was extremely important to me. You see, in order to be able to carry a gun as a retired police officer, it had to be endorsed by my law enforcement agency. My law enforcement agency could only endorse me if I was considered honorably retired as defined in the California Penal Code. Police officers like myself that are terminated are not considered honorably retired. There was a little known section in the California Penal Code that set up a three-member panel that would establish if I met this criteria. Their decision was final and non-appealable by the LAPD. So if I was able to convince a three-member panel that I did not deserve to stay terminated but instead be classified as honorably retired, I would not only get my badge, police identification, and lifetime pension, but have my permanent status changed to be an honorably retired police officer. No longer when asked by my students at the university or by people I meet that I am a former LAPD officer who was terminated for making a mistake on an audit. I could simply pull out my badge and identification and say I am honorably retired LAPD. Period. That was huge for me. However, be my hearing was to take place along came Christopher Dorner.

The "Dorner" Effect

❖ ◆ ◆ ◆ ◆ ❖

On February 3, 2013, a series of shootings began in Orange, Los Angeles, and Riverside counties in California, in which the victims were law enforcement officers and civilians (including law enforcement families and those who were misidentified as the suspect). Christopher Dorner, thirty-three, an involuntarily terminated Los Angeles police officer, was named as a suspect wanted in connection with the series of shootings that killed four people and wounded three others. The rampage ended on February 12, 2013, when Dorner died during a standoff with police at a cabin in the San Bernardino Mountains. A manifesto posted on Facebook, which police say was written by Dorner, declared «unconventional and asymmetric warfare" upon the Los Angeles Police Department (LAPD), their families, and their associates, unless the LAPD admitted publicly he was fired in retaliation for reporting excessive force.

While I cannot condone the method Dorner used to seek revenge after the LAPD personnel who he held responsible for his termination, there are some ere similarities between his case and mine. His retaliation began after he reported his training officer for misconduct. Mine had two components: reporting misconduct by employees that were stealing and having sex on duty (lesbians) and then eight years later reporting my supervisor for having sex with his commanding officer in the police station parking lot and then abuse of the departments computers and confidential information that led to an eleven-year jail sentence. According to the Los Angeles Police Manual, employees are mandated to report anything that may be considered misconduct. However, often times when you do, they come after you with trumped up charges. Boards of Rights are made up of two LAPD command staff level employees, e.g., Captain, Commanders, Deputy Chief, Assistant Chiefs and one civilian, often an attorney who is neutral. The burden of proof is preponderance which is not hard to prove for the Department. Basically fifty-one percent. The decision does not have to be unanimous. Just a majority or two to one decision. This of course, gives the Department the advantage because they can totally ignore the civilians position even though they are the only unbiased decision maker outside the system. Also, normally there is a higher ranking LAPD command staff employee paired with a lower ranking command staff. So a captain is not going to go against a deputy chief even if he or she believes that Chief is wrong. Quite often the civilian on the Board of rights votes in favor of the officer.

I don't know how Phil Tingirites or "tits" as we use to call him ever got to make the rank of captain. I spent one year playing on LAPD's semi-professional football team traveling the country with Tingirites as my head coach. I won't go into details but I am quite sure he has terminated employees at Boards of Rights that have done less than he ever did. From my personal perspective and things I witnessed him do, I do not exactly think of him as a man of integrity. This is my personal view. It is not unusual for personal and professional conflicts to be allowed to stay in place during LAPD Boards of Rights. In his manifesto, Dorner wrote, "I later went to a Board of Rights (department hearing for decision of continued employment) from 10/08 to 1/09. During this BOR hearing a video was played for the BOR panel where Christopher Gettler stated that he was indeed kicked by Officer Evans (video sent to multiple news agencies). In addition to Christopher Gettler stating he was kicked, his father Richard Gettler, also stated that his son had stated he was kicked by an officer when he was arrested after being released from custody. This was all presented for the department at the BOR hearing. They still found me guilty and terminated me. What they didn't mention was that the BOR panel made up of Capt. Phil Tingirides, Capt. Justin Eisenberg, and City Attorney Martella had a significant problem from the time the board was assembled. Capt. Phil Tingirides was a personal friend of Teresa Evans from when he was her supervisor at Harbor station. That is a clear conflict of interest and I made my argument for his removal early and was denied. The advocate for the LAPD BOR was Sgt. Anderson. Anderson also had a conflict of interest as she was Evans friend and former partner from Harbor division where they both worked patrol together. I made my argument for her removal when I discovered her relation to Evans and it was denied."

None of this surprises me. LAPD Boards of Rights were notorious for terminating police officers—even if there is contradictory evidence. Another uniqueness between Officer Dorner's Board of Rights and my own was that he had Captain Justin Eisenburg as the other Command Staff Officer on his Board of Rights. If you will recall, Captain Eisenberg was the same Captain that came after me when he first came into Pacific Division. I made a fool and a liar out of him and it wasn't that difficult. First he got jealous because I had a better parking spot than him which was the handicap spot. It was so petty that he spent hundreds of hours and tax payer's money to investigate my injuries including violating state and federal HIPPA and Americans with Disabilities Act (ADA) only to conclude that in his medical opinion I didn't qualify to be able to park in a handicap spot. The only problem was that he wasn't a medical doctor. I had a field day putting together a rebuttal affidavit including a list of all my injuries, which all happened on the job, doctor's opinions, medical records, surgical records. The California Department of Motor Vehicles letter authorizing me to park in a handicap spot, etc. I sent copies to my attorneys and to the Los Angeles City Attorney's Office. I am sure he was read the riot act form the City Attorney's Office. However, what he did next instead of swallowing a big piece of humble pie and admit he was wrong embodies the mentality of these LAPD command staff officers who think they can do anything to ruin careers and lives with no recourse. So after having to admit that despite his best effort to prove that I was not injured and therefore was not legally entitled to park in a handicap spot, he did a complete U-turn and one-eighty. As I already discussed (supra).

Getting Out of God's Way

I have been in "attack mode" with LAPD since 1995. I have been through so many challenges to my career, my health, my life, etc., that when I am faced with yet another challenge from LAPD I go into a zone. I start thinking like a lawyer and prepare my case and think of strategic ways to attack and come out victoriously. The same was happening in the instant case. Given that I only had a few weeks to prepare for probably my most important hearing since joining the LAPD twenty-five years before, it made me all the more focused, aggressive and intent on winning. My wife told me that she was deeply worried about me because she knew how much it meant to me to get my CCW, my badge and more importantly my reputation and good name back. The thought of losing, she surmised, might push me over the edge into severe depression. She might have been right. I started to wrestle with God. He kept telling me, not audibly, but impressing upon my spirit strongly, to leave it up to Him. To trust Him. You would think it would be easy trusting God with this issue given how He has delivered me time and time again. Miracle after miracle He has led me through valleys and low, arid places. However, my personal hatred against what the LAPD and the City of Los Angeles management had done to me and my family had evolved into a personal war. I wanted so bad to beat them and show them they were wrong in coming after me that as I said before, I quit my PhD which I had already started and put myself through law school in order to learn how to fight back. I had also been very successful at it. There was something else that motivated me. I have, from time to time, run into former LAPD officers who were wrongfully terminated like me. Several have been my actual students at the University of Phoenix where I taught the undergraduate and graduate programs in criminal justice. When they come across someone who has gone through the same defaming as them, the same corruption and devastating effect on their careers and good name, it is extremely cathartic. Several have literally wept while telling me their stories. I fight for these individuals as well.

I have been told from an attorney in the Los Angeles City Attorney' Office that no other employee has had as many victories, settlements, and positive outcomes against the City of Los Angeles in the history of the City of Los Angeles as me. There it is again—pride. It is so easy for us to take away God's glory. The Book of Judges and the story of Gideon is a good example of God works so He can get the Glory and not us. Gideon had assembled an army of thirty-two thousand men to take on the Midianite Army of approximately one hundred thirty-two thousand men. God, knowing man's penchant for taking the glory for themselves, had Gideon dismiss ten thousand soldiers from his army. This was still too many for God. God then had Gideon dismiss all but three hundred men through an act of battle readiness. Gideon now stood to take on an army of one hundred thirty-two thousand Midianites with only three men. This was more than a four hundred to one advantage for the Midianites. God knew however, with this few number of Israeli soldiers only He could get the credit for the victory. Most of us know the story of how each soldier carried a lit lamp inside jars of clay which they smashed and blew trumpets which sent confusion into the Midianite camp and they slaughtered each other.

The point is that God wants His glory. So it was in my situation. Here I was again faced with another critical adversarial hearing against LAPD who never plays fair. The Lord was putting on my heart and in my spirit to trust Him with this hearing. I couldn't let go of it. How sad is that? So the Lord had to do what was necessary in order to get me out of the way. He struck me down with an illness. Now I have to qualify this statement by telling you that I don't get sick. I almost never, ever get colds, the flue or any illness. My four kids come home from school all the time and sneeze and cough on me but I don't get sick. Up until this time, I don't think I had been ill in over five years, maybe more. So about ten days before the hearing when I was running around trying to call up possible witnesses, drafting legal points and authorities, and generally stressing out, I got sick. A mystery illness. I still don't know how to describe it but I was bed ridden. With me out of the way, God was able to now go to work behind the scenes.

As discussed, this hearing was going to be made up of a three-member panel. One individual was to be chosen from the Los Angeles Police Protective league otherwise known as the LAPD union. One member was going to be picked from LAPD management. This is the member that troubled me the most. The last member of the panel or board was supposed to be a neutral member. They came from a list of independent members that the city kept. Most of them from my experience were attorneys. These panels were not as formal as LAPD Boards of Rights or Boards or Boards of Inquires, for example. There was no substantive evidence offered or evidentiary witnesses called. Instead it was more inquisitional in nature. I was however, allowed to have a few character witnesses which would be questioned by the board. One individual I had chosen as a character witness was Mike Morlan. Mike was well known and a Detective III which is the highest LAPD rank a detective can have. Close to the rank of lieutenant. Him and I also were both professors at the University of Phoenix and taught criminal justice classes together. We also worked as partners when we were young bucks in the Department. I also picked Sergeant Lane Bragg as another character witness. Sergeant Bragg was one of the greatest LAPD officers and sergeants I have ever had the pleasure of knowing. A Vietnam veteran with great survival instincts, he spent his entire career helping other officers by stopping citizen complaints in the field or representing officers accused of misconduct. It probably cost him any higher rank. He became very upset at my termination (he was a witness for me at my Board of Rights). He was so upset at the injustice that he immediately, after the Board of Rights was over, with the finding that I should be terminated, went to the chief of police to file a protest because he knew the Board of Rights was a sham and that even if what they claim I did was true it wasn't even misconduct never mind a firing offense. The departments advocate must have known were sergeant Bragg was going because Sergeant Bragg was met at the Chief's Office by two of the chief's adjutants (lieutenants) who told him point blank that they knew why he was there and that he should know that "Barry Brooks was terminated for reasons other than what he was charged with and to go away." The fact that they openly admitted to fraud, false charges, and lying to a department supervisor tells you how much confidence they have in no one holding them accountable. Management doesn't like supervisors who defend or otherwise try to keep officers out of trouble. The whole mentality back then was for supervisors to "burn them to learn them" so when a sergeant goes before the command staff trying to make lieutenant he or she can brag about how many officers they have taken complaints on or burned. In fact, I personally know of an officer who committed suicide whose family would have been denied the officers life insurance policy if not for Sergeant Braggs fortuitousness. Enough said. Lastly, I chose Philip Kaplan. He was my lawyer in several of my lawsuits and appeals. He knew how screwed over I had been by the LAPD. He had worked for the union defending police officers and filing lawsuits against the city of Los Angeles. He had a pretty good reputation as a bulldog. He took on cases in which his clients were clearly the underdogs. Although we didn't win our appeal from my termination which was handed to him after two other lawyers had butchered it, he even got a superior court judge to say on the record that "Do I believe that Barry Brooks has enemies within the LAPD management? Yes, I do. Do I believe Barry knows who they are? Yes, I do." So there they were. My three character witnesses that I hoped were convincing enough to persuade at least two out of three panel members of the hearing panel that I should be honorably retired, with all of the rights, privileges, and vestments that came under the Law Enforcement Act of 2004, be given my badge, police identification with CCW endorsement, as well as having my status changed from a terminated employee to an "honorably retired one. I had already appealed and won my twenty-year lifetime service pension as mentioned earlier. The date for my hearing was now set, the players were set and the venue was set.

Leading up to the date of the hearing, December 3rd, 2013, I had been trying to make contact with my former lawyer and character witness Phillip Kaplan. I really thought he would make an impression to the board. As a lawyer who had personally deposed some of the LAPD command staff involved in my discipline and my termination and promotional hearings, he could show the unfairness in which I had been treated by LAPD management and the duplicity and hypocrisy I had suffered at their hands. Some of the things he uncovered while deposing them would make your stomach turn. Filthy, immoral, and defiling acts. These were the same command staff officers that sat in judgment of officers like me and terminated officers for minor infractions while they committed felonies and behaved in ways that would make a sodomite blush. He also knew the ins and outs of my termination and knew it was bogus. As an officer of the court, I thought he would come across with credibility and neutrality. However, Phillip earned his law degree from Tulane University in Louisiana. He had license to practice law in California and Louisiana. I had been calling and emailing him since October with no response. I knew he was involved in a civil trial in Louisiana but I was just trying to inform him of the hearing that was mostly going to occur in December and then once I got the actual date, of the date and time of the hearing. I sent him over a dozen emails and phone calls. As it got close to the hearing date, I started to lose heart a little bit figuring that he was the only outside character witness. My other two witnesses were both LAPD employees. The day before the hearing he called me and said he had just got back from the East Coast and got my message. He said he would be there.

I really didn't know what to expect during this hearing. A lot of my previous hearings with LAPD I felt were predetermined and I was simply wasting my time and energy preparing a plausible defense when they were going to find me guilty anyway. So I started going into these hearings and using them as a way to make a record for the courts. The only time I received justice was when I went to an outside arbitrator such as state or federal judge. Judges rely upon transcripts of administrative hearings to determine fair play. Even though LAPD had a habit of losing recordings and transcripts, it was still the only way to get justice. Consequently, when I was first brought into the board and introduced I almost immediately went into a long apologetic of the LAPD discipline system. I wanted them to know the extent of abuse that had now, in 2013, lasted eighteen years. The way LAPD paints me in my personnel package is pretty bad. They ignore the order to remove a bunch of complaints and they remove all of my awards and metals and commendations and make me look like a chronic complainer and incompetent. On top of what I felt was a burden to prove to the board that I was more of a victim of LAPD retaliation, I was told by the sergeant who was in charge of putting the hearing together not to be emotional. He said part of the Board's decision besides determining your honorable retirement status was giving me the ability to carry a weapon. Under HR 218 or what is known as the Law Enforcement Act of 2004, President Bush gave the authority of any honorably retired police officer from any state to carry his weapon in any and all fifty states. Also, I would be exempt from California's ban on high capacity magazines and weapons. In the back of the board member's mind was the nightmare scenario that they go ahead and grant an officer his badge, police identification and endorsement for Carry Conceal Weapon (CCW) permit and they go out on a rampage and kill people. I imagine it is kind of like being on a Parole Board and paroling someone who within a month of being released kills again. The same thing that torpedoed Governor Michael Dukakis' bid for presidency in 1988 when he gave weekend passes to murderers and violent criminals. One such person was Willie Horton who, while serving life in prison, received a weekend pass from Governor Dukakis and then proceeded to kill a young boy, stab and old man and rape his wife in the getaway.

The emotional strain of eighteen years of battling for my career, my family, and ultimately my life, had taken an emotional toll on me. It was difficult to retell events from my past with LAPD without all of the emotions coming flooding back at once. Because it was one long, never ending chain of events, I think my mind and my emotions couldn't bifurcate the events. One story told about an event that happened fifteen years previously would trigger a memory that had partitioned all of it into one giant bad memory. It was kind of like the Dutch boy who put his finger in the dike. Eventually it will all come flooding over. So not only did I feel I had to convince the board that I was a good guy who got a raw deal and it was up to them to right a wrong, but I had to do it while not getting emotional. Great. The chairperson of the board was a female manager from Human Resources Division. This is who I feared most. She started off by reading the rules and how the hearing was going to proceed. When she got done with the introduction and I believe she was going to launch into the beginning of the hearing I stopped her. I said, "Excuse me." I apologize for the interruption but stated "I would like the Boards permission to give an opening statement. "I could tell by their quizzical looks and response that this was something they had never encountered before. I spent about ten minutes pleading my case. I did an overview of all of the retaliation starting in 1995 and continuing through the city's recent attempt to deny me my lifetime service pension. However, it was when I discussed to the Board that the LAPD not only went after me but went after my wife by singling her out in the police academy and locking her in a room without food, water, or bathroom use until she would agree to quit the LAPD that I started to lose it. When I recalled that event from 2003, I started to lose my composure. I had to wipe a tear from my eye and quickly turn my head and pretend like I was having allergy symptoms or something along those lines. The echoes of Sgt. Mendoza's warning "Don't get emotional!" was my silent focus.

By the time I finished my discourse to the board, I could tell that I might have made a mistake. Maybe the members of the Board were not out to get me after all. I couldn't tell but I felt that I threw them off balance by my opening statement. I had also provided copies of my settlements to the board to prove to them that certain complaints were not supposed to be in my file and therefore shouldn't be considered when reviewing my personnel package. I think they felt some paranoia in my behavior. I was just do use to defending myself and having my package purged of all good things and the bad which was supposed to be removed left in. So it came time to bring the character witnesses in. This meant that I had to leave the room. I went down the hall way to the waiting room where I was to wait along with my three character witnesses during the hearing. They called in Sergeant Lane Bragg first. Sgt. Bragg and I go back a long way to when he was the Senior Lead Officer of Beat 14A14 which was a gang infested area in Venice. I was loaned from where I was working in South Central Los Angeles to Pacific to work that area called the Oakwood Gang Task Force. He taught me how to develop informants and treat people right—even gang bangers. Later he promoted to sergeant and supervised me for over a decade and knew me better than anyone else. He wrote many of my ratings and representing me during complaint investigation interviews. He knew that the department had been out to get me since I exposed the lesbian society and through the next thirteen years of retaliation. He came back from testifying kind of quickly being led by Sgt. Mendoza. He walked into the waiting room and we all kind of wanted to get his feedback on what went on inside the hearing so we could prepare for any questions that might be thrown at us. He told us that they had only asked him two basic questions: 1) How do you know Barry and; 2) do you have any problem with him carrying a gun? That was it. I was hoping that Sergeant Bragg would be able to get into more detail about the years of persecution that he had personally seen me go through as my supervisor. He was also the individual that the Chief of Police's adjutants told that I was fired for another reason than the actual charges that were brought against me at the Board of Rights. He was one of the few percipient witnesses that had actual knowledge of the Los Angeles Police Department's not only history of retaliating against me but actually giving an admission that they had fired me on trumped up charges. This is how cocky they are. When I won my lawsuit forcing them to promote me to sergeant and detective, the lieutenant in charge of administrating the legal settlement's orders was bragging that they didn't care what the settlement or what the court said. They were going to not just deny my promotion to sergeant and detective (for the third time) but get rid of me. Now here they are terminating me for what doesn't even amount to misconduct, using evidence they weren't allowed to, and then openly admitting it was all a pretext to terminating me. This type of share contempt for the administrative system of justice comes from a systemic attitude and culture that they can burn whoever they want even if it is totally unjustified and without merit because they know they will just keep getting promoted up the chain of command.

Next to testify was my friend and former attorney Phillip Kaplan who had handled my termination lawsuit and knew the history of the LAPD's relentless retaliation against me. Also, he was an attorney for the Los Angeles Police Protective League, he had successfully fought against the LAPD management and had deposed many of them. His intimate knowledge of how the department goes after anyone who defies its authority or questions its veracity was important. So Philip went in and like Sergeant Bragg, was brief. He came out of the hearing and told me that he told the board that I had been the victim of a relentless effort of LAPD management to harass, retaliate, and do everything to get me to quit until they finally had to make up a charge and fire me. He pointed out that my appeal of my termination that while not successful was a very difficult threshold to prove (manifest abuse of discretion). Only about one in ten officers win Writs of Mandamus on appeal because of this threshold. He also pointed out that the judge himself who had read the transcripts of the Board of Rights and the appellate brief acknowledged that there was probably someone in LAPD management that was retaliating against me and that I probably knew who it was. Quite an ominous statement coming from an impartial judge who sits on the bench of Los Angeles Superior Court.

My last character witness was my old partner and current colleague and professor at the University of Phoenix. He had promoted up to Detective III which is just below lieutenant but above sergeant. I actually broke him in on the streets of Los Angeles when he was a rookie. We had a lot of fun. We stayed friends and I had recruited him to work in the criminal justice department with me at the University of Phoenix. Mike went in to testify and like the others, wasn't in there for more than five minutes. He came out and walked down the hall were the rest of us were sitting in a small waiting room. Now came the wait as Sgt. Mendoza said that the panel was now going to deliberate and discuss my fate. I had dreaded a negative decision. It is easy to see sometimes in other people's life how maybe their faith wanes and ebbs and flows. Here I was, sitting in a waiting room, about to find out one of the most important decisions in my life—at least career wise to me. God had already given me an incredible track record of miracle after miracle. He had done so many supernatural things in my life, showed me favor and His grace, that I felt a little ashamed that I was still worried about the outcome of this panel. Still, we are human. How many times have we read in the Bible about the Israelites or David or Abraham failures of faith right after God had done so many wonderful and miraculous things in their lives? Maybe I was being hypocritical. It is easy to look at other people's lives and say "just have faith." In Christian circles we like to throw around Romans 8:28. God works all things for the good of those who love Him (paraphrased). It is such a simple construct. Yet here I was at a critical juncture and my faith was lacking yet again. How sad. We Christians do have short memories and I also think that we quickly forget the blessings around us that God has provided like a job, a roof over our heads, children, health, food, etc.

It didn't take too long for a verdict to be reached. Sgt. Mendoza told me that the Board had come to a decision and escorted me by myself back into the hearing room. I sat down and gave a quick eye contact to try to get a quick read on the mood of the panelists. The female manager for the City, whom I was the most worried about, wouldn't make eye contact with me which I thought was not a good sign. Then she spoke. She was still looking down and said to me, "The Board only has one thing to say to you," she said in a somber tone with her eyes still looking down at the table. This can't be good I thought to myself. I prepared myself for the worst news possible. Suddenly, she thrust her hand out at me and with a big smile on her face said, "Congratulations!" I shook her hand still in disbelief. No LAPD hearing had ever gone my way despite the evidence. It was always pre-textual in nature. The other two board members stood up and reached over the table and shook my hand as well congratulating me. They told me it was a unanimous decision— all three members voting in my favor. I was then ushered out of the room and down to the waiting room where my friends who had testified were anxiously waiting. I walked in and yelled "I won!" They all stood up and started patting me on the back and shaking my hand congratulating me. I broke out in tears and started sobbing. It was embarrassing but the flood gates of years and years of abuse and emotional frustration that had been buried deep in the recessions of my mind suddenly had an outlet. I could tell some of the guys weren't sure what to do. They have probably never seen another grown man weep. A police officer especially who is trained to put a wall around his/her emotions because we can't show them when we see people burnt alive; heads cut off; children raped and strangled and all of the countless other things we see working the streets of a city like Los Angeles. It probably didn't seem like a big deal to them and it wasn't in the grand scheme of things. However, to me, it meant everything—especially my reputation. Now I could say I was no longer a terminated employee of the LAPD. Now I was an honorably retired police officer with all rights and privileges. Under the Law Enforcement Act of 2004, I could now carry my gun in all fifty states and my badge would now be emblemized with a stamp at the top of my retired badge stating honorably retired. Then the female manager of the City of Los Angeles came down the Hallway and walked into my room and gave me a big hug and once again said congratulations to me. Sgt. Mendoza said to me once she left the room, "Wow, I have never seen her do that before to anyone." A few minutes later, another of the panelist and board members, Lieutenant Lally, came down the hallway and sought me out. He walked up to me and told me that this was a no brainer. The entire panel had agreed that I was victimized by the LAPD and voted to give me this win. What came next from him really threw me for a loop. He looked at me and said something like God was watching out for me or words to that effect and that he too was a Christian. He told me if I ever needed anything at all to give him a call and he handed me his business card, shook my hand and walked away. Within ten minutes, the room cleared out and I was taken downstairs and had a new honorably retired police identification card made with the words "CCW endorsed" on it. I filled out the paper work right there to get my badge changed to honorably retired and for my retired certificate and plaque. It was like the fastest two hours of my life. I was literally dazed and confused. I was joyous and thanked God but I was walking on cloud nine over the enormity and suddenness of what just happened in my life. As I took the elevator down to the street level where I had parked my car I started thinking about everything that God just did to get me that victory. He got my attorney witness to finally call me back the day before the hearing. God arranged it so that he could get a last minute flight back to Los Angeles and be able to testify at my hearing. Also, God arranged it so that the third panelist, who was an attorney, that was chosen out of a dozen possible panelist, was an attorney who personally knew my attorney. What are the odds! Just as strikingly, God had arranged for my friend and former partner that testified, Mike Morlan, to be promoted and then transferred to the very LAPD unit that was responsible for making judgment calls on whether police officers should be able to carry a handgun or not. This was the only thing to seem to really worry the Board. Granting me honorable retirement status meant giving me the ability to carry a weapon by their authority. What would happen if I then went out and killed someone with that license they had granted me? So when my friend Mike testified for me and they found out that he was the officer-in-charge of the Mental Evaluation Unit and by default the department expert on this issue and he told them he had no problem with me carrying a handgun, they were off the hook. They could now say that the LAPD expert in this area approved of them issuing me the ability to carry a concealed handgun and no longer have to carry that burden. Also, God arranged it so that Lieutenant Lally, a God fearing man, was on my Board. Just a God thing again.

When I got out on the street, I was so mentally and emotionally wasted that I had temporarily lost part of my memory. I could not remember where I had parked my car just three hours before. I knew it was parked somewhere on a city street within a few blocks of the building I was in. However, I literally had no memory of parking it just hours before. I had to force my memory to remember what kind of car I drove and I have owned my Tahoe for twelve years at that point. I walked around the block. I then walked a two block perimeter in a square. I then walked a three-block perimeter to no avail. Nothing looked familiar. I started to think it might be stolen or towed. I was determined not to let this issue ruin what an incredible day it had been. I stopped on the side walk and implored God to help me find my car. I prayed He would reveal where my car was located to me and also thanked Him with tears at the same time for the victory. I started walking, turned the corner and there it was! I got into my car and realized that I had not told my wife yet. She was very worried that if I lost my hearing that I might sink into a deep depression and be even suicidal. She kept telling me not to worry if I didn't win but she knew after being married to me for twenty years and personally seeing the agony of what I went through and what she went through that it would be very hard on me. I was in my car and just sat there crying. It was more of a thankful cry. It was a release of eighteen years of emotional turmoil (1995-2013). I didn't want to call my wife on the cell phone because I was simply not composed. I was a mess and really unable to say anything coherent but mumble some thank you's to God as more emotions poured out of me. So I sent her a text with two words: "We won!" I started driving home and she called me back about ten minutes into my drive back to Orange County. I picked up the phone and without saying a word she just broke down in tears and mumbled something inaudible. I tried responding back but then I started weeping loudly again. We both tried to speak to each other but it was just lots of tears and thank God's. A few days later, she surprised me with a cake and the words "We won!" written on top of it. The whole family celebrated the victory.

Am I Going to Die?

I would like to end this book in the last chapter with the great victory from the Lord. However, I believe that Lord was still teaching me a lesson during this phase of my life. The truth is, I was dying. I was being slowly poisoned but didn't know it. Often times God tries our faith by either sending or allowing hardships/trials into our lives. What good is untested faith? How do you know how strong it is until it is tested? They say that faith is like a tea bag and that you never know how strong it is until you get into hot water. After my near-death experience during surgery in 2008, I was diagnosed with some pretty severe heart ailments. My injection fraction ratio was measured at 45%, normal being around 60-65%. My heart was enlarged, left ventricular not working properly and I had arrhythmia. About two years later, I started having what some doctors called seizures. It didn't matter where I was or the environmental factors. All of a sudden I would feel sort of a coldness coming over my both, a sense I was losing consciousness and it felt like I was suddenly oxygen deprived. I would start taking deep breaths thinking that it might go away if I could get enough oxygen in my system but that never worked. Next, I would have an almost out of the body experience—sometimes being able to see myself as my spirit was leaving my body. My left arm would go slightly numb and I would then start smacking my lips together as I was aware of what was going on around me but not able to fully respond. A few times I had episodes while speaking and my speech became slurred. After the episode, I would experience nausea and fatigue like I needed to lie down and rest.

These episodes would occur on a regular pattern. I would have two to three a day, lasting about one minute and I would have them for about seven to ten days straight and then they would disappear. They would go away completely for about three weeks with absolutely no systems. Then one day, almost like clockwork, they would come back two to three episodes a day for about seven to ten days and then go away again. The neurologist had me try Keppra, an anti-seizure medication. However, I simply could not tolerate it. I simply felt like a zombie while on it. I tried it twice and just couldn't handle it. The interesting thing about anti-seizure medications is that they just don't know how they work. I asked the neurologist and the pharmacist and they both said that the medical community really doesn't know the mechanism as to how they stop seizures in the body. Since I had already been seeing a cardiologist for my heart after the surgery incident, my cardiologist thought it was related to my heart issues. Nothing worked and I learned to live with them. Much like Paul the Apostle prayed for the Lord to take away his ailment (thorn in the side), I prayed the same. However, the seizures, diagnosed by one neurologist as "complex-partial seizures and syncope" would remain. I don't have to tell you the challenge of having a seizure attack while driving. Post-LAPD I was teaching for the University of Phoenix all over Southern California and would often drive between one hundred fifty to two hundred miles round trip each day to reach each of the twenty different campuses. I had to feed my family. So this issue of seizures made things more complicated. Although I never actually lost consciousness during the seizure episodes, they were still distracting. I normally would get about a twenty-second lead time while driving before a full-episode onset. This lead time allowed me time to pull over most of the time. However, Southern California traffic being what it is, it is just impossible at times to get off the freeway safely that quickly.

I, like many Christians, when facing adversity sometimes wonder if it is from God or from the enemy. I think far too many Christians blame the enemy (Satan) for the results of the natural consequences of their own sinful behavior. Look at what King David had to live with after Bathsheba. The devil made me do it offers up a very convenient excuse. Instead of recognizing our own sin and confessing it to God we blame the devil. At the same time, I also think many Christians think of the devil more of a cartoonish figure who is more imaginary than real. One thing I know for sure is that God is in control of the Universe and our lives—the life of the believer. So if God is in charge of the universe and if he is omnipresent, omniscient and omnipotent, then certainly nothing can happen in the life of the believer without God allowing it. That is an accurate and biblically sound truism. We also have Romans 8:28 to remind us that "God works all things for our good to those who love Him." So now I had my thorn in my side much like Paul and I had accepted that fact until October of 2014. From my experience, I usually know when I am doing the Lord's will because I come under fire from the enemy very intensely. He is not foolish either. He knows our weaknesses, our vanities and how to get to us. Often times he uses the weaker vessel in our lives like our wives, children or in the case of being unevenly yoked—the unbelieving spouse. As I have consistently stated through this book, the Lord called me to write this book and He confirmed it four times. So in October of 2014 when I knew I had to put some time aside to complete this book and do God's will, I did so without hesitation. I had prayed a few months earlier in anticipation of taking some time off. My goal was to take the first three weeks of October, 2014, off from working to finish this book. Knowing this would be difficult to do financially, a few months earlier in July, I asked the Lord for $20,000. I figured I would let my wife spend $10,000 getting the master bathroom remodeled which had been in a state of disrepair after we hired some incompetent contractors to remodel it. It ended up costing us more than double what they told us and the work was so shoddy that the City Building Inspector wanted to red tag my house because of the exposed electrical wires they left hanging all over the bathroom. We also needed some other minor repairs around the house that had needed fixing for a long time. So I thought that along with my small pension and teaching part-time at the university I would be able to use the remaining $10,000 to live off of and pay my bills during the three weeks I was planning on taking off. Then the enemy made his move.

As I discussed, I had by this time, been having about three years' worth of seizures that have affected my health. I had grown somewhat accustomed to them but the ancillary effect was not good. My blood pressure had gone from 118/72 to 210/110. These seizures were annoying and a little scary as I literally felt like I was dying for about a minute. I had an appointment at the beginning of October to go see my cardiologist at the much respected Cedar-Sinai Hospital Cardiac Center. This was on a Friday. I was also scheduled to go to Irvine for two days (Friday to Saturday) and assist the San Diego Christian College with developing and creating a new leadership bachelor's degree program based upon Christian principles. Leaders and intellectuals were flying in or driving from all over California in order to make this meeting happen. They were holding the meeting in Irvine, so it was only a few miles from my house. Later I found out that the nearness of the location was done as a convenience for me. Thus, I felt obligated. San Diego Christian College is located way down in Santee, California, South of San Diego and about one hundred miles from my residence. Two days before I was to drive up to Beverly Hills to see my cardiologist (Wednesday), I had another round of seizure episodes. This time they were different. All of a sudden, instead of having about two a day on average, I had six on Wednesday. Thursday I had eight attacks. The attacks were much more severe and debilitating in nature. I don't know quite how to describe them. All of the same symptoms were present as a normal attack but just much stronger. The next day, Friday, I was scheduled to drive to see my cardiologists. Normally I would have had my wife drive me but she was busy taking care of her parents. I was on the 405 freeway just north of LAX Airport when the attack hit. It was sudden, almost no warning unlike before. I was driving about 65 mph which was the speed limit and traffic was moving pretty good. When the attack hit, I did the best I could to stay alert but I definitely did not have time to pull over this time so I had to ride it out. At one point, I had to sort of slump over the steering wheel of my car while gritting out the sensation of an existential experience. I am not quite sure how long my attention was averted but I think only a few seconds before I recovered. When I lifted my head up,

I saw a frightening sight—traffic on the freeway had come to a complete stop and I was still going 65 mph and the gap was closing fast. My immediate judgment sensed that at my speed combined with the stopping power of driving a 5,000 SUV truck, would allow me not stop in time. Instinctively, I made a quick jump to the lane to my right without looking which thank God was not immediately occupied by another vehicle. This lane had another seven to eight car lengths distance before the vehicle was stopped in front of me. I hit the brakes as hard as I could and heard for the first time anti-lock brakes actually lock up. I actually could see the panic on the driver's face in front of me reflecting from her review mirror as she also heard the noise of my brakes lock up and from her look apparently didn't think I would be able to stop in time. Fortunately, the Lord spared me what would have been most likely a fatal or near fatal accident.

I continued driving to my cardiologist office which took another twenty minutes or so. I was in his waiting room when all of a sudden I had another seizure attack. For several years I have had to explain to my cardiologists my symptoms over and over and even wore a heart monitor twice but could never capture one of the episodes in his presence or on a monitor. Towards the very end of the attack, my doctor walked out into the patient waiting area and looked at me. He said, "Are you okay? You don't look good." I didn't have a lot of strength to talk because these seizures temporarily zap me of my strength. I managed to whisper but in a shouting manner, "I just had an episode" as I was hunched over. He looked very concerned and gave me a cup of water. He seemed very concerned and opined that I was pale and ordered the nurse to take me to an exam room and immediately hook me up to an EKG machine. About five minutes go by and my blood pressure was 230 over 120. My pulse was one hundred fifty beats per minute. This is five minutes after the end of the attack. I cannot imagine what is was during the attack. Maybe two hundred beats per minute? Maybe this is why I feel like I am dying. My cardiologist wanted to admit me in the hospital at Cedar Sinai immediately. However, I would not let him because I was due at the conference for San Diego Christian College in Irvine within an hour. Up until this point, my doctor and I had been fighting with LAPD workers' compensation to get them to pay for an MRI of my brain and EEG of my brain to rule out that the seizures were not being caused by some damage to the brain. In 2006, I was hit in the head by a metal baton and had a concussion. I had pretty severe vertigo and was actually leaking fluid from my brain out my nasal passages. It happened on the job so it was automatically worker's compensation but I stipulated at "0" which means no money for the injury but should have included lifetime future medical treatment covered by the City of Los Angeles. I had been trying for almost a year to get the City to cover these tests but the Deputy City Attorney who I had taken to court over my unpaid worker's compensation benefit kept preventing the approval of my treatment.

The following day I went to Cedar Sinai Hospital emergency room by advice of my cardiologist. He had admitting privileges their so he wrote up the orders and told me to report to the emergency room and they would admit me and per his orders conduct and MRI of my brain and EEG of my brain. The doctors in the emergency room were positive that something was wrong with my brain (as my wife has been telling me for twenty-four years). They thought I might have brain cancer, something wrong with the wiring of my brain—a kind of short circuiting if you will. However, in the emergency room the doctors told me that they couldn't get me to the labs for the MRI and EEG until the next day and I would have to spend the night there in the hospital. They got me a room and I was willing to stay the night so I could finally find out what has been causing these seizures all this time. However, the emergency room doctor told me that since my condition wasn't acute, since I didn't come in the emergency room in the middle of the attack, my insurance probably wouldn't cover it (Obamacare of course) and I would be looking at a $20,000 emergency room bill. My wife and I discussed the fact that we were already in debt and getting by paycheck to paycheck that we really couldn't afford this kind of debt so I checked out of the hospital and made an outpatient appointment for both the MRI and EEG of my brain in two weeks.

What I didn't realize was this emergency room doctor felt he had an obligation as a mandatory reporter and notified the

California Department of Motor Vehicles that I shouldn't be driving with my current condition. The following week I got a letter in the mail from the California Department of Motor Vehicles (DMV) that they were ordering me to literally get my head examined by a neurologist. Having a driver's license in California is a necessity. Most people I know that live out here commute and average of fifty to sixty miles a day. I spent my last ten years with LAPD commuting about one hundred miles a day round trip. The last five years as a college professor I was commuting, depending on which campus I was teaching at, up to one hundred eighty miles a day round trip. My car has almost three hundred thousand miles on it. Also, the fact that I was still actively seeking employment with law enforcement made it worse because you cannot drive a police car without a license or even hold that position. There were also the possibilities that the doctors were right and I had a brain tumor or something wrong with the circuitry in my brain which could be fatal or require surgery. To add insult to injury, we had been ripped off by some shady contractors and lost $10,000. The university had also forgot to put me on the fall schedule so I had no income stream coming in. The Department of Motor Vehicles made me be cleared by a cardiologist, then have a complete work up of my brain with an EEG and MRI of my brain by a neurologist before they would let me drive again. Even though I passed all those tests, I was still having seizures. Then the DMV made me see a psychiatrist before they would allow me to drive. How embarrassing. The psychiatrist didn't know what to do with me and so she put me on some powerful anti-depressants. Something that would elevate the serotonin levels in my brain. Again, like before with the anti-seizure medication, Keppra, I couldn't function on the medication. I was like a zombie from the night of the living dead. I had now been suffering from these seizures and accompanying symptoms for five years. I had been through a plethora of tests for my heart, brain and mental well-being with no answer.

By the time 2015 rolled around, there were still no answers. I prayed a lot about it. I had lost the job of my dreams as a lieutenant of police working for a personal friend and chief of police because of my condition and knew no one in law enforcement would touch me. I was now coming up on my fifty second birthday and wanted to bench press 500 lbs. for my birthday as I had did for my fifty first and fiftieth birthday as part of a goal for my life. Probably not a good idea as I had already torn my left shoulder labrum, both biceps, both ulnas (forearms), left calf, both quadriceps and tore my abdomen open until my intestines came out. Never said I was smart. As you could probably guess, I ended up tearing my right should labrum at two locations as well as my rotator cuff. I had immediate surgery. I didn't realize at the time but God allowed me to be stupid in attempting to bench press 500 lbs. (vanity, vanity!) in order to save my life.

The moment I woke up from surgery, my orthopedic surgeon looked at me kind of quizzically. He looked right at me and said, "Are you taking minocycline?" I asked him "Why?" The doctor answered and said, "Because your bones are as black as charcoal!" The answer was yes. I had been taking minocyline for about ten years just to control some small acne break outs I got on my back once and a while from sweat soaked t-shirts clinging to my skin during frequent weight-lifting and cardio sessions at the gym. It was more for summer time at the beach when you take your shirt of and want clear skin. More vanity than necessity. Still, I took the medication all year long. Year after year. After all, what's the point of building your body up to be 260 lbs of muscle with 8% body fat if you can't show it off once in a while (vanity, vanity!)? Turns out that that vanity was killing me.

Little did I know that recently doctors had discovered a host of side effects, some life-threatening, caused by long-term use of minocycline. Before the heart problems started I had discoloration on my feet which I was told was caused by problems with my skin pigmentation. My fingernails had a bluish hue to them which I was told was due to low oxygen in my blood. I was diagnosed with hemochromotosis with toxic iron levels in my blood. My creatin levels from my kidney were off the charts. My liver function was way off. My gums were grayish in color. I kept tearing different muscles and tendons. I had high blood pressure after years of it being normal. Headaches, seizures, intracranial pressure, gastrointestinal disease requiring numerous surgeries, hiaital hernia, respiratory issues, fatigue, narcolepsy and of course now I knew that all the bones in my body are black in color. These were just some of the problems I was experiencing over a decade of taking this medication which I had attributed to stress. No one tied the two together. Not my general practitioner, not my cardiologist, not my phlebotomist, not my neurologist, not my dermatologist. No one. I made and appointment with my dermatologist to try to confirm this diagnosis. I didn't end up seeing him but his assistant, the PA-C. Her name was Randee and she and I had been friends for a long time. She told me that the dermatologist I was seeing just got sued for prescribing this same medication because it was now well-known in the medical community the side-effects that minocycline was causing. I immediately ceased taking the medication. Within six months my seizures were totally gone, blood pressure back to normal, discoloration of the skin was going away and just about every major symptom I had been having had gone away. I went to see a specialist not too long after and he told me that I was lucky to have had such an astute doctor because in his opinion I would have been dead within a year had I kept taking the medication. It's funny how God works sometimes. After I tore my shoulder, I had scheduled surgery with an orthopedic surgeon who had worked on me before when I tore my left bicep about a year earlier. However, even after I booked the surgery, I simply didn't have peace about it. God sometimes gives you a wrestles spirit when He is trying to guide you away from making a decision out of His will or one He knows is wrong for us. He just impressed upon my spirit to go to another surgeon. I contacted my insurance and inquired about other orthopedic surgeons that did shoulders and I was sent to this doctor. He actually wrote a book on the very type of surgery I was going to have. Feeling comfortable with him, I switched surgeons—a decision that saved my life. God saved my career, now He saved my life.

The Future

❖·❖·❖·❖·❖

I don't know what the future holds for me here during this earthly life but I do know who holds the future. I am still waiting on God to fulfill His promise He made to me via prophet back in 2010 to "do something new in my life." I have always felt, and more increasing so now, that that next chapter of my life won't take place until I accomplish the task at hand—this very book you hold in your hand. I think it is quite ironic that as I sit here and write the last few pages of this book taking me three years of my life, that the very man responsible for a lot of misery in my life is now being sued by the Los Angeles Police Protective League for violation of due process and civil rights of police officers under his command. As he is finding out now, you can't hide from your sins, they will discover you out.

Many people struggle with understanding what God's purpose is for their life. Many Christians do not seem to take the time to be alone with the Lord, to learn to hear his still small voice and to enter into a relationship with Him. We are his children. The analogy that I often give when speaking about my faith whether on radio, at universities or even one-on-one mentoring, is that of a biological fatherhood. Most people, not all, have a love and respect for their earthly fathers. So I would ask them a hypothetical question: if they turned eighteen, moved out of the house and never ever called, wrote, or otherwise communicated to the earthly fathers again, would their father be sad? "Of course," most people respond. Then I would tell them that it is no different with their heavenly father. He loves His children and wants to enter into a relationship and dialog with us throughout our lives. He wants to communicate with us and spend time with us. How can we ever learn God's plan for our lives if we don't allow Him the opportunity to tell us? This is one of the biggest questions that plague us Christians. What is our purpose in life? Who wants to go through life never really knowing what God put you on earth for? Yes, we can generalize and say that God's purpose for us is to be conformed to Christ through the Holly Spirit and this is true. Being a Christian is serious business and it is a lot more than just going to Church on Sunday and tossing an envelope into the plate. God doesn't want our money but our hearts. I think that the biggest regrets many Christians are going to have is when they get to heaven and realize just how many opportunities we missed in serving the Lord that He had in mind for us but we simply wouldn't give him our attention.

People do ask me if the eighteen years of hell that I went through with LAPD was really worth it. If I had not done the right thing and did not report all this misconduct, I was aware of and simply looked the other way perhaps I would be a Captain in the LAPD right now making $150,000 a year with a chief of police job somewhere in the future. The truth is, in my heart, this is how I wanted my life to go. However, God used the hardships in my life, many brought by Him for the purposes of maturing me and teaching me to trust Him. My hardships, sufferings, and of course incredible triumphs by God has allowed to me minister to other people in ways I simply could not have if I hadn't gone through these trials. What better purpose in life is there to be used of God, the holly sovereign of the universe to get His will accomplished? The fact that He includes us in His salvation plan for the world is mind-boggling. If God can use me, believe me, He can use anyone to get His will accomplished.

About the Author

B arry Brooks grew up the quiet suburbia life of North Reading, Massachusetts before moving to Los Angeles in 1988. His law enforcement career has included the following agencies: Army Military Police, Essex County Sherriff's Department, US Marshals Service and twenty-five years with the Los Angeles Police Department. Barry has also worked for the Department of Defense, Office of Chief Trial Counsel, California Supreme Court, and interned with the Los Angeles District Attorney's Office and the Los Angeles City Council. Barry has been a graduate professor of law, criminal justice, and homeland security for over twenty years at several local Southern California Universities and has appeared as a panelist on Appologetics.com Christian radio program on KKLA. He currently owns and operates his own private investigation business and is an active volunteer at his church, Calvary Chapel, Costa Mesa, CA. Barry has earned the following degrees: Juris Doctor Law, Master of Science Criminal Justice, Master of Arts Organizational Management, Masters of Arts Faith and Culture, Master of Science Communications, Bachelor of Science Criminal Justice and Associates of Science Criminal Justice. He is married to his bride for life Nevine for over twenty-two years and has four children: Rachel, seventeen; Mark, sixteen; Sarah, ten; Elizabeth, eight.

CPSIA information can be obtained
at www.ICGtesting.com
Printed in the USA
FSHW01n0712080618
49188FS